Dear Roger,

So great you w'—

me of this special day —

Erica Sarzin-Borri—

"Artist Erica Sarzin-Borrillo has written a memoir that informs as much as it inspires.

Her shared early memories from her childhood- filled with, as she describes- love and craziness, up to her most recent reflections on the challenges of our pandemic fueled days, are all wrapped in the wisdom that in the midst of difficulty we can still find joy and inspiration!

Chasing Radiance may be one person's recounting of a life inspired, and directed by spiritual oversight, yet while the details may differ, it is truly the story of us all.

Erica encourages us to open our eyes to the higher octave that is ever present in our lives."

- Selina Maitreya
Transformational Agent/Author
www.practicalspiritualitywithselina.com

"Erica takes us on a very unique journey, often defying the gravity of our limited beliefs and experiences. Her artistry is radiantly reflected in her touching memories, her soulful art and her mystical musings. Clearly, diversity can be transmuted into mulch. I walk away inspired to paint my own life."

- J. Tamar Stone, M.A., C.H.T.,
Senior Voice Dialogue facilitator, Creator of Selves in a Box,
and author of Body Walk Meditations

"Recounting her rich and multifaceted life, mystic, artist, and raconteur Erica Borrillo takes the reader on quite an adventure. In retelling her colorful and well-lived life, she shares her inner as well as outer journey; through childhood challenges, her career as an actress, her marriage and family life, as well as her struggle with severe illness. Throughout, Erica offers inspiring spiritual insights and metaphysical reflections drawn from her dreams, her study of the Tarot, C. G. Jung, Jean Houston, and many others."

- Gary Toub, Ph.D.
Diplomate Jungian Analyst and Spiritual Mentor

"I have known Erica Sarzin-Borrillo for 50 of our almost 70 years, and have never ceased to be amazed by her creative gifts and endless generous offerings to the world in song, dance, drama, writing, teaching, art and artistry of all sorts...

She has always represented – for me – the ultimate creative life. The divine muse is her essence, her lover, and her way-shower.

I have found this book entertaining, inspiring, and impossible to put down! Erica's writing style is vivid and the stories in her journey – some dark and fearful and some wildly exhilarating – are rich and fascinating.

All who seek to know the heart and soul of the artist will find sweet nourishment in these pages.

Savor and Enjoy!"

- Jane Smith Bernhardt, author of "We Are Here: love never dies"

and "The Sweet Conversation: a guide to spiritual listening"

Founder of <u>Listeningcircles.com</u>

"Erica has written a brilliant, poignant memoir. I loved every minute of it. She is a great story teller and reminds us all that bringing our authentic selves to the world is essential."

- Cynthia James - International Speaker and Best-Selling Author

"I Choose Me: The Art of Being A Phenomenally

Successful Woman at Home and at Work"

CHASING RADIANCE

CHASING RADIANCE

MEMOIRS & MUSINGS

By *Erica Sarzin-Borrillo*

BALBOA.PRESS
A DIVISION OF HAY HOUSE

Balboa Press books may be ordered through booksellers or by contacting:

Balboa Press
A Division of Hay House
1663 Liberty Drive
Bloomington, IN 47403
www.balboapress.com
844-682-1282

Because of the dynamic nature of the Internet, any web addresses or links contained in this book may have changed since publication and may no longer be valid. The views expressed in this work are solely those of the author and do not necessarily reflect the views of the publisher, and the publisher hereby disclaims any responsibility for them.

The author of this book does not dispense medical advice or prescribe the use of any technique as a form of treatment for physical, emotional, or medical problems without the advice of a physician, either directly or indirectly. The intent of the author is only to offer information of a general nature to help you in your quest for emotional and spiritual well-being. In the event you use any of the information in this book for yourself, which is your constitutional right, the author and the publisher assume no responsibility for your actions.

Any people depicted in stock imagery provided by Getty Images are models, and such images are being used for illustrative purposes only. Certain stock imagery © Getty Images.

Print information available on the last page.

ISBN: 978-1-9822-6993-7 (sc)
ISBN: 978-1-9822-6995-1 (hc)
ISBN: 978-1-9822-6994-4 (e)

Library of Congress Control Number: 2021911961

Balboa Press rev. date: 06/11/2021

Dedicated To

My husband Paul who believed in me when I lost confidence.

My son Shane who has blessed my life with his presence.

&

To family and friends of my Soul

CONTENTS

Cover photograph by Denny Bitte   ✦   *Graphic design by Karen Neville*

And the Goddess said to the traveling fool:
"Listen well to the Wind that calls your name for destiny
reaches out in mysterious ways...

Beloved Journeyman, I say this to you now, for your worries may become too much at times to bear: take joy in the process of life. Remain open. Remain curious. And always be willing to begin again! The path is not always clear. Sometimes you will find yourself spinning in circles or leaping into the unknown, only to discover that you left valuable pieces of yourself behind in haste. Begin again with courage and compassion for the sake of your soul, the soul of humanity and all beings large and small. These are powerful times of global disturbance yet rising consciousness. New ideas are in the making, new languages are being formed, and new paradigms are coming to be. But the world has been out of balance for so long that the crises mankind faces now demands far greater dreams and solutions than ever before.

So go forth, Adventurer of life, and fiercely dream the World anew... Trust the magnificence of your mission dear Fool, for there is reason for your being... You are the Hero of your own great tale that has flowered from the beginning of time. You are the One and you are the Many. Look at the living symbol that is your life and let it be your lead, for this is the Sacred Dance, this is the Sacred Stage!"

INTRODUCTION

*"For small creatures such as we
the vastness is bearable only through love."*
Carl Sagan

What are we to do with the existential weight of our human condition? I am an elder now as I put these memories and reflections together. But there is a certain thread through my life that keeps me on some soul path and some soul mission despite whatever fates seem to have interfered. No, alas perhaps fate is more like destiny's fuel… and urges us to be ourselves first and foremost.

I admit to falling under the cultural spells that have little to do with the ideal course of our lives or with the ultimate question: Did we succeed or fail while dancing on this tiny pebble in the sky for such a short while?

If we leave it to the current culture, we miss the mark on why we came here as unique individuals… because in the end, the culture would have us conform, keep up with the Jones's, buy into and thereby willingly absorb mass belief systems that set us up against each other and confuse even the simplest truth… that we came here to become ourselves… to filter consciousness in our own unique way… to respond to the whole shebang as tiny as we are in this infinite cosmos… to come alive fully with passions of all sorts because that is how the human can hope to become one with the Gods. Yes, the best of one's life, at least of mine, is a spiritual matter. And in that, my sense of success is almost always in the ever unfolding now and in the creative birthing of beauty and in the Seeing of beauty even when it seems lost in the darkness of the times.

I've been through a lot in my life. And the current culture would have me bury it away and diminish it. But I think the culture is not the way of the soul. I believe a well lived life is one that has given credence and the highest regard for our life's myth. And if we can't honor our past Sacred wounds, scars and all, we will never have truly lived and loved. And we'd better at least give a valid try at both before we die.

At those pearly gates I hope God's sentiment will translate well: What a fascinating life you led; Sacred wounds and all were delivered poetically as well they ought to have been. But most significantly, the effort you put into this life is most appreciated. Whenever a flower blooms then falls away yet blooms once more, it grows the world with love.

Before I speak of stories, art, or even contemplations, let me begin by saying this: I started my memoirs 11 years ago but didn't feel the timing was right. It was a time to reflect of course as reflection simply comes with the territory of being a conscious man or woman. We are all journeymen are we not? And somehow journaling that grand journey of ours seems a natural need as we leave our crumbs along the way. Even so, I was never one to note my history in terms of facts (though my memory is startlingly long. I remember as far back as one, perhaps even before one.) I tend to speak poetically, existentially or soulfully if you will. You'll find a good deal of that in this book. In any event I've always been a prolific artist of many sorts and have written an embarrassing number of plays, poetry, and books worth, though have only published one. I've produced much but like many artists, my studio is spilling over with oh so many splendid ideas and unfinished works. So at this late date my aim is to, as artistically as possible, lay much of it out before you along with whatever "words of wisdom" I've gathered along the way.

The synchronicity around this publication is rather uncanny actually. A vision came to me one morning recently of a book fused with memories, reflections, and philosophical essays. But almost as soon as

2

that vision came to me so out of the blue, I dismissed it, thinking it might just result in one more barrel of unfinished scraps of scribble. Apparently however, the "Universe" had no intention of letting me off the hook so easily. You see, no more than a few hours after my vision I was approached by my publishing company to write a second book. And so here we are. I signed the contract even though I didn't have the manuscript… Sometimes "the calling" comes by way of such synchronicity and though you may or may not follow through, the truth is you've no doubt been in dialog with your highest good. Quite possibly you were being offered signs that suggested so if only you had listened and acted upon them. I must admit, I have merged many philosophies into my own special concoction, I suppose. And it certainly seems that Mystic laws have been at work in my life from early on. Synchronicities have been extraordinary directives in my life and through my life. And when I've lost my way, as we all do, I turn to the Tao and such to remind myself of the almost magical nature of life. The Universe of which we are an integral part will find its way to spell things out.

Now this: Two weeks after I signed the contract to publish this book, however, I experienced quite a dramatic event and was lucky to get through it. Had I waited I might not be here to tell my tale… literally. I evidently contracted a virus that may have gone to an already weakened heart and to be honest my life changed overnight. I was rushed to the hospital via ambulance and was told I had a life-threatening condition and would be on meds for the rest of my days. Time would tell how they'd get me on my feet… if they could get me on my feet.

Of course, you might question my sanity when I say the timing continues to be just right for memoirs when my energy might be compromised for a follow through on such a project. But you see, I'm not only transitioning into my later years when folks begin to think of leaving their stories behind. I'm transitioning with immediate and compelling focus and with a need to touch my son, my husband, my friends and anyone who might possibly be moved. Life or death situations will tend to do one of two things: they will render you helpless with the feeling there is nothing left to "fight for "or they will fuel your will and destiny somehow. Well, I suppose you could say

I've always had a strong will, and an even stronger need to "speak my truth". I'm not too often struck down by entropy, thank goodness.

Beyond all this, I see little commodity in putting up scarecrows to chase away reality. I don't mean to say that I'm a stoic by any means but my heart is unstable, and I don't honestly know what will be. But I suppose there's something within me that is simply too hungry for life to let my life force down. The truth is, I've had heart issues of all sorts from the beginning and so there's no denying they are indeed part of the fabric of my life, and therefore part of my story (as has been the case with Lyme disease). It's rather a miracle I've kicked so many traumatic health problems many times over. However, if there was a calling to live my destiny, I believe the Angel of Death was quietly resting upon my shoulder right beside my destiny. It was he who ushered me in and it is he who has been waiting by patiently to usher me out.

I lost my beloved mother when I was 12, she just 39. And although I already had an uncanny sense of the creative unconscious from the start, losing my mother so soon brought to me the raw truth of eternity and finality all at once. I've been grappling with that paradox head-on since childhood and no doubt it gave birth to the mystic within. It never ceases to amaze me however, that I have outlived her, particularly because of the numerous times my angel called on me. Despite so many extreme health issues I've had, I nonetheless feel oddly supported by Spirit and Soul.

As far as the rest is concerned, I find myself "letting go" in ways I might not have in my youth, yet simultaneously longing as usual, for one more crack at beauty. So, here I am. And with regards to this book of memoirs and such, I know that mine may just be one more story to be carried forth but this is how we spread our seeds and hopefully our own special wisdom. They say "We were born to these times". I believe it is so very true. We give the world our word through an individual story that is ultimately hooked to the Universal, so as far as I'm concerned it is something of a mission to share along with the rest of our gifts that perhaps we were meant to give away!

James Hillman stated long ago, we are coded from the beginning just like the acorn which holds the coding of the full-grown tree. Well, a

4

mentor of mine used to point out to me that he felt I was born to be an Artist… that I fell out of the womb that way. And yes, it was no doubt true. But it is my belief that the way the world falls into place for each and every one of us, is the result of fate and destiny and no random turn of events. I was enraptured and captured by the arts from the beginning and lived in the tower of the artist's life, devoting myself to all that meant… because of what was "meant to be". Certainly, once I began tapping into "the creative unconscious" I found an insatiable need to dabble in as many arts as I possibly could. I was lucky "to find my bliss" as early as I did because it offered a medicine to my soul through "a difficult childhood". And it has remained a potent medicine for the growing of my soul through the years.

Most creatives would agree that there exists a kind of mythic or spiritual storehouse one has access to while painting, sculpting, singing, dancing, writing, etc. etc. etc. and as such we can taste the realm of eternity; of Kairos time. I pause as I say this to you and remember my early obsession with the idea of infinity. Oh yes… such are the possible musings of a baby artist.

Such artistic engagement even for a child just becoming conscious, can open the portal to a rather potent conversation, certainly with one's muse, and hopefully with the divine. Perhaps this is why so many of us are philosophers and even mystics at heart for there's no denying the deep spiritual component to creativity itself with the ability to step aside from ego and allow the soul the right to soar.

I thank God, I found my way to the arts. Certainly, I was led by the spirit of creativity to the door of personal story, where the possibility of individual and collective healing resides, along with the Soul's greater message to Humanity (and maybe even to the Universe itself!). Hopefully by the end of our days, we will know of the gifts we came to give and we will know as well what we came here to say, having lived our own legend; a legend both Unique yet as vast as Infinity itself.

So onward, sometimes by way of reflection, sometimes by the voice or hand of my muse. This, in any event, dear reader is my humble offering: my story, my ancestry, my art, my feelings, "My Life".

I

TIME PAST; THE ANCESTORS

I was born Jewish, though I know little of the religion. It is the people, "my people" that I feel connected to and I feel our "Jewish condition" strongly. Perhaps it is because my mother and her family came to America during the war, that the Holocaust seems as present to me as it does. I am truly moved by my family's personal stories, and can't help but hold the experience of those terrible times somewhere in my heart.

We are more than our lifetime of course. In fact, we are connected to the family of man eons old, from past, present, and quite possibly the future. And though we rarely consider it, our ancestry is ancient. I have always found that notion to be most compelling, particularly when you think about the number of great great grandparents who lived before us and still remain within our blood and within our souls and within our DNA. We are one small spec within our ancestral family.

How, with this in mind could I write my personal story without including what I know of my ancestors? I've seen little of my extended family of cousins and such through the years. And I regret that we are so scattered. But there is a history of which we all are part and I find that a powerful element of my life.

Years ago, I did a few Department of Defense tours entertaining military families abroad. It was a marvelous way to see much of the world I might not have seen otherwise. And I thank Heaven I spent at least a bit of time in "ancestral Homelands".

On route to Germany, we drove over the Alps that brought us through some of Austria; my mother and Grandmother's place of birth. You can call me a romantic and you'd be right. But nonetheless, I feel a resonance in my heart with places such as these. And I feel blessed to have experienced that brief encounter with Austria on route to Germany. There, I also experienced a deep but odd resonance, or rather I should call it an empathic recognition with a place I'd never actually been to. Indeed, what I experienced was a visceral, palpable awareness in my bones that I'll never forget. We'd spent one of our days off, at a preserved concentration camp. I believe it was considered the smallest one in the town of Flossenberg. I hardly know how to speak of it. Everything had been preserved and left intact, that is of course except for the people who lived and died there, yet I felt their spirit still remained alongside the gas chambers and burial sites. I walked very slowly through, taking it all to my heart. The one thing that struck me was the uncanny juxtaposition of the pristine beauty of the land in contrast to my awareness of the savage nature of these killing fields. How devastating is the Jewish condition whether you are religious or not. We are a people who have taken the brunt of outrageous prejudice while far too many held the insane belief that the world needed to cleanse itself of the vermin called Jew. Yes, we are all part of the great family of man, but our Jewish condition is indeed carried within our DNA, in the Quantum field, and in our Souls. And many of us born thousands of miles from the Holocaust, nonetheless, know the strange phenomena of survivor's guilt. Thank God my mother's immediate family fled to America, the land of the free, the land of hope and blessings for all who sought the highest ideals this country offered with arms wide open. Those were the days of American grace on the heels of insanity and rationality turned upside down. It's worth looking back to track the many oscillations of our pendulum swings. But of course, that is another story, isn't it?

My mother along with her siblings; Sybil (written in the international passport as Sybilla, known to us as Aunt Billie), Guido (Uncle Guy), Aunt Eleonore, and my grandparents, Hilda and Papa Sam escaped via ship safely and began a new life. As the story goes there was another who died aboard that ship. I seem to recall that I knew the facts behind this event but have lost the details. I do know she never completed the voyage and for all I know, she jumped ship. In any event I've been haunted these many years about her passing. It has "inspired" me in many ways and hooked me… connected me to my people, our plight, and I suppose in some way, my own stance in life which is to be an agent of transformation in ways large or small. I suppose we are still learning about love and will have to keep on doing so.

There are family stories that were passed on to others that I never heard. And so, I decided to reach out to my sister and cousins to see

9

if they might share what they themselves knew. Even with that, one can't be absolutely certain of the facts the older you get unless the facts were recorded early on. Some of the stories are subtly different as told by different family members and some are wildly different. It seems my recollection of my poor relative is vastly different than what I only recently learned. Perhaps we are all meant to make our myths a work in progress, which little by little are layered by imagination or by a deeper truth trying to express itself. Look, in any event, these stories and impressions are important, perfectly factual or perfectly imagined. After all, we are the keepers of our tales of yore.

Here are some of those stories. I shall begin with a few letters back and forth between me and my maternal grandfather's cousin, René Gelman, who was heartfelt enough to explore our family tree and to stay in touch when this family scattered. I am most appreciative of his interest in our history and I suspect to some degree he and I are both romantics as well as artists, so it may be within our "sappy" nature to bring some of these stories to light.

THE LETTERS

Dear Erica,

First, I'm happy to read your thoughts on the family "clan" as you say. Second, I hope that your heart problems on which I've read in your former messages, you've managed to solve them on the way to keep them in the mental, that is also important, and not in the biological domain.

Regarding your interest in family, I'm happy that you, probably the only one pay attention on our family tree that I conceived sometimes ago.

Not everyone accepted the way it was made and suggested other formulas that could be found online. Of course, I'm not a specialist into this problem, however, I prefer my way, because myself being tight to graphic expressed ideas, I think that everyone just as a glimpse of this tree are able to see the position of every member of the family in relationship to each other and in time. On what you are posting about the Bayer's "clan", my observation is that the Bayers is just one part of the family. The oldest one that I mention into my work is the one that gave the family its name, Gelman, family that stretched today from the South America, Chile, to North America, Canada, passing through Romania, Germany, France, Italy, and the United States.

You mention Billie, whom I heard when I was a teenager, talking between the "oldies" at that time. However, what remains in my memory, if it's true or gossip, is that the name Bayer, has its origin in the business that one of the family, that, after emigrating from Latvia on racial/religious persecution, to Romania, established in the town of Galati (Galatzi). Its business was that of the public bath, that in Romanian language, (which has Latin roots) is the word Baier. From Baier to Bayer, is a matter of adapting to the language of the world into your lives.

Related to this, I remember a story that with the many years passed over got the "flavor" of the legend, is the one of my cousin Joseph

(Yoji) in the family, with spouse Paola. I can remember them well when they leaved Romania, on board of the ship, one of the passengers told them that with the name Baier, if a little bit changed, more American style, in Bayer, they could find more easily a way to get a job. If it's true or not... who knows.

PS. Like every time when I send a message, I'm apologizing for my bad spelling. English is not my "Muttersprache". Actually, is Romanian.

René

Dear René,

This is beautiful and authentic with spelling "issues" and all.

Do you still have the tree you made? Also, please explain who you were to my Papa Sam.

Forgive me, but I don't recall. Are you cousins? And you, like many of us are an artist of course... an architect, yes?

BTW, I heard a story of a relative who fell or jumped off the ship to America. Do you know of this story?

Love, Erica

Dear Erica,

First, I start to try to answer your questions in your January 30th. Email, beginning with the last one, the one about someone of our family that "landed" by accident or not at the bottom of the ocean.

In one of my last conversations with Sophie Campitelli, that is the sister of your Grandpa Samuel (who we the family called him Buby), she told me that her mother Anna (born Ghelman than married Bayer) contemplated to visit her French family in Marseille. "Traveling by ship across the Mediterranean Sea from Bucharest, via Constanza and the Black Sea, she fell sick and died. According to the rules of navigation, the commander ordered that the body should be thrown overboard into the waters of the sea. This story after many years was confirmed to me by her son, Andre. At the other of your questions, if I did well understand it, your Grandfather, Papa Sam as you called him, is, was, my cousin. His mother, Anna, and my father Lazar, were siblings. Their age difference is maintained between that of Sam's and mine.

Regarding my work, there's a little story as well. Mom being "Eine practice Berleiner", believed that her son (me) due to his inclination towards drawing, should choose a more practical profession than that of being an artist painter. She knew that from her own life experience. And that was the architecture.

Fortunately, after the end of WWII, Romania fell into the communist countries of Eastern Europe. I mention "fortunately" because in the matter of choosing a profession, in socialist ere, tuition for the five years of Architecture study was free. The parents couldn't afford to pay it for their son in a non-socialist regime. Well, there were another "fortunatelys". Being Jew, on those times in Romania's fascist country, everyone who has one Jew parent is considered Jew. During three years of war, I have to be enrolled in the "forced labor", that means that every half day I worked hard non payed at the needs of the town hall, and in the afternoons, school. For a teenager starting life this way, was hard to accept. So, then I became Communist. I had a chance to get a job to make projects for the highest level of the Central Committee of the Romanian Communist party members, and as such, I had the opportunity to know a little bit about the life of those "high level comrades". Comrades that according to the French comedian Colluche who said that "we are all equal, and some are even more equal than others", enjoyed life in the buildings that I designed. One was a villa on the board of a lake, in very well guarded forest domain, far away from public view. Today it is used only for the government diplomats' foreign guests. But the "fortunatelys" continued with my story. As an architect, paid by those "equal high members of the party", being able to think about my membership to the Communist Party, I thought that something didn't fit with the Communist "moral" life, and criticized it. Result? I was "excluded", thrown away from the CP as a "Party's enemy". A friend of mine made the same "faux pas", and after three days after his arrest, his family was noticed to take home his body, because he died of "unknown causes".

So then, dear Erica, being aware of my long, much too long "logorrhea", I'll speak of two buildings that I've designed. The first is an apartment building in the center of Bucharest, with a view of on City's most beautiful gardens, and another one that is the dome of the state circus in the capital town of the Mongolian state, Ulaan Bataar. It was in 1975 originally painted in pale blue, to fit the

Mongolian Hills landscapes, but now they painted it in gold... without asking me!

Dear Erica, if you managed to read all that letter, I thank you!

Best health wishes, René

Hello René,

Forgive me. I'm trying to make out the names on the family tree. (tiny print on my end) So I can't see all of Sam's siblings. He was one of 5, I believe: Sami, Yoji, Theodore and his twin Sofie, and... I may be wrong but I thought there was a sister named Feetsa... and she lived in Marseilles and also has a son named André. Am I confused? If you could set me straight, I'd appreciate it.

Thank you, Erica

Erica,

According to "my" tree there are 5 of Anna Bayer's kids: Samuel (Sam/Buby), Joseph (Yoji), Hans, Sophie and Theodor (twins). Sam built his family in the USA, Yoji in Argentina, Hans and Theodor moved to Israel, Sophie married a French (Italian) in Marseille had a son André and daughter Diana (she died some years ago)

You say Feetza, maybe a confusion of name if it's about Sophie. Within family there are many nicknames that sometimes could have a background. In Romanian language Feetza (Fita) could be one of them. As long as I know, based on family gossips, Sophie had an adventurous life. There appeared the name of one of her lovers (married or not) Peppy , whose origins were with the Check Republic. Maybe her family named her about this adventurous kind of being, that the word Fita characterized it. I didn't find the right translation in the dictionary, but the meaning is closer to "capricious woman". Why you do not contact directly her son in France... Marseille. We are very close each other since many years. He does not speak English. He is very "French". However, by email you could have a conversation. I've just a short telephone talk with him and he gave me permission to give you his phone and email.

My Best, René

At this point, I'd like to say that evidently when one is attempting to dig through a history like ours, though the conflicting stories can be fascinating, it does take patience. I begin to see the detectives' process which doesn't come quite naturally to an artist type... or indeed the process of historians. Eventually with all this, a time line and more clarity will come to pass. In the meantime, I must admit, I perhaps like you, the reader, am longing to know a bit more of my Grand Aunt, Sophie/Fitsa and my Great Grandmother, Anna... and so I did reach out to André and gratefully he answered.

Dear André,

We met many years ago with George, Mado's son from her first marriage. René and I have been in touch as I'm writing a book and am looking for family history for one of my chapters. I'll be grateful for whatever you might have to offer. I remember some stories of your mother, who I knew as Fita... I didn't even know her name was Sophie. Someone actually said she hid people as part of the resistance. Is this true? (so many mixed-up stories)

Also, when and how did she die? I'm sorry for my confusion on this matter.

I am so happy to be in touch and hopefully you will be as happy to engage a little on the subject of our family.

My best to you,

Erica Sarzin-Borrillo

Hello Erika,

First of all, I would like to know two things: your mother's first name and what happened to George the son of Mado. Regarding my mother, I think she was an adventurer and very free for her time. In 1941/42 she was rounded up in Paris by the police because she was Jewish. Then she was locked up in a camp in the so-called free zone in the southwest. At that time, France was divided in two, the North occupied the Germans, the south administered by the French collaborators. She escaped to cross France and arrived in Marseilles in the South east. It was my father who hid people in the hills around

15

Marseilles. She was never in the resistance. In 1944 I was born, then my sister in 1946. I married in 1977 to Christiane and we have 3 children: Laurence's, Cecile, and Jerome. Mom lived with us in our property of Cadolive near Marseille. Sick of heart she was the last month of her life in a convalescent home and she fell. She broke her femur, like your Grandfather. She died on the operating table in 1988 at 83 years of age. I had no contact with my family in Ursa, probably because of the language barrier, unlike that of Romania which I am very close. I think you are familiar with and therefore you can send me your questions, and the machine will translate them. That's what I did. I'll wait for your email when you want.

André

André,

So good to hear back from you. You are already clearing some things up but there is one story that remains muddled. I wonder if you might tell me more of Anna who died on board a ship crossing the sea. I'm sorry to say Mado died many years ago of a terrible cancer... she was planning to live with us in Colorado. A month later she was gone. And then George died of cancer a few years later. My mother was Mady. (Madeline) Tragically she died when she was 39 years old and I was a young girl. I am writing my second book which will be a smorgasbord of musings, memoirs, and some family history... and hopefully a companion book of my art. I guess as we age this kind of reflection becomes a turn on the path. So, I thank you again for reaching back out to me.

Blessings

Erica Sarzin-Borrillo

Erica,

To come to the death of our Grandmother Anna on this sad boat, I personally experience this painful period for my mother (whose first name was Sophie and the friendly diminutive Fitsa)

When the family split up before the war, your Grandfather was in different European countries. Italy, France, etc... My mother, Sophie also before leaving her husband and living with your Grandparents in

Paris where she was "beaten up" by the police, otherwise she would have gone to the USA with your grandparents and all their children. The three boys (Joseph, Theodore and Hans) stayed in Romania with their wife and mother Anna. After the war (1946/47) the communists took power and Romania was behind the "iron curtain". Joseph called Yogi and his wife partly escaped on foot and arrived at my parent's house in Marseille. But the period was murky and finally they preferred to go very far and immigrated to Brazil.

Then remained the two brothers who each had a daughter and Anna Bayer (your Grandfather Sam's mother), my mother (Fitza), and the others (5 children). In the 1950's Romania softened. For payments by the state of Israel, it a seized the opportunity and left. Anna found herself alone and Sam was very affected because he loved his mother so very much.

She finally managed to get an exit permit for Israel and joined her two sons. With the help of my mother, Sam then obtained a permit to bring her to France. But she was very old and had Angina (heart disease). At that time drugs were very sketchy. Air travel was not democratized at all. People were traveling by ocean liners.. Anna took the boat from Tel Aviv to Marseille. Sam paid for a first-class trip but we thought that the fatigue of the trip and her emotionality caused her to have an angina attack and she died on the second day of the 5-day trip. The captain did not want to keep the body and she was sent to sea as was the custom on boats at that time.

I was eight years old, my sister six and for us the arrival of the grandmother was an event. We were very disappointed. But my mother had a serious nervous breakdown and I, a young boy was very afraid that she would die for two years.

I must admit I do not know any of my first cousins because I have been to the USA only 3 times in the family. Once at Mado's in Dumont and once at Sandy's in Washington DC. Then for the celebrations of the bi-centenary of the French revolution and the aid of France to the Americans in 1789, two days at Daniel's in Sam's house in 1989. On the other hand, I went with my wife and my children to Canada in Toronto, in Quebec, and in Vancouver where everyone speaks French. My wife never wanted us to go to Israel for security reasons and I don't know my relatives there. I can give you more details about my mother, who was a little "sulphureous" in the family. Reasons for leaving Romania after marrying a childhood friend older than her. Of the life he gave her in Czechoslovakia before she left him to join your grandparents. Then Hitlerian madness on Europe which destroyed everything. It was this period that my parents lived through and that your grandparents and their children were able to escape, even if your mother's death was a tragedy. My mother often talked to me about it. My correspondence was a little long, I apologize. You can see on the map of France my mother's trip during this war. Paris Bordeaux (the camp was 80 km south of this city, then Marseille on the Mediterranean coast at the start of the French Riviera. I have a lot of photos, Sam and Duchy in Paris with Guy, Mady, and Sandy, and great photos of Guy's marriage to his first wife. Photos of Leon and Anna Bayer in Galatz (Romania) by whom it all started.

Finally, tell me about yourself. It seems to me that Mado had told me you were doing theatre, but over time, I may have confused.

I kiss you, André

My dear André,

I am extremely moved by your letter which brings this family/ancestry to me in a real way. Yes, I am in the theatre or shall I say I was… I'm needing these days to "exercise" calm due to my own heart issues. (It seems it has run through both sides of my family)

Incidentally, my husband and I spent an amazing time 5 years ago driving from Florence, to the south of France, into Spain. At the time I had no idea how to get in touch with you. I regret that.

BTW, in this chapter on family history, I'm using email conversations with several cousins etc. I'd like to include these if you don't mind. They tell things well and are truly compelling.

Thank you, thank you, thank you.

Erica

THE INTERVIEW

To speak further about my mother's family line, I turn to the set of tapes my sister, Stefani recorded in the 1970's. She and her first husband, Barry, visited our Aunt Billie, as we called her, in Washington DC and conducted a full-on interview over a two-day period... There was much to tell that we girls knew very little of. Some years later they were made into CDs but I recall that they were nearly impossible to decipher when I first received them. Fortunately, technology has certainly improved since then. And with the aid of new devices, the words came through and so I went about translating them as best I could. I wanted to stay as true to the stories as I possibly could, short of offering up the actual question/answer transcripts.

Once again, I want to be clear, as my own sister pointed out, that some of the stories are factual, but some are no doubt translated through Billie's experience... She was the oldest of the Bayer siblings and held the history of the family when others had either passed or were hard to reach. I am ever so grateful to my sister for the initial interview. aside from René and André's letters, The Bayer chronicles might have been lost on the winds without it. I found Billie's account compelling, often charming, and quite dramatic particularly when it came to the family's experiences and eventual escape to America during the war.

I also became increasingly aware of my ancestral connections as well... regarding such things as health for instance, artistic talent, and even personality traits. I might add that upon hearing the tapes after all these years, Billie's voice, Continental accent and all, was remarkably present and alive. I'm sure you can imagine how truly uncanny it felt... almost... mystical!

My people were nomads, but then again, generally speaking our tribes were known as "The wandering Jews" and apparently wandered throughout history. The Bayers were originally from Finland, then immigrated to Latvia. Eventually they left, due to religious persecution and settled in Galetzi (Romania). There's a little something of the Bayer personality that resonates with me to some degree as it was no doubt "handed down." I'm actually proud to take it on despite the "shadowy" aspects of it. Sam was said to be deeply independent, almost "willful". I would rather use the term "passionate" which to my mind covers a lot of territory and gives a different picture to the kind of person some might think of as "a trouble maker"! I suspect he had what I like to think of as "a warrior spirit". But, Billie herself used the word, "Bad". Yes, she said Papa Sam was very very bad and was thrown out of schools for his very bad behavior. Well, of course I didn't know him in his youth. I wasn't born but I remember him well in his later years and I will say this... He obviously grew out of his wild days because as far as I'm concerned, I never in my life knew a finer gentleman. This is true. I imagine Sam was a restless sort perhaps even a kind of soul searcher... a seeker for the kind of life that would bring him meaning. And he would leave his home and family to do so. He did graduate from The Constantinople College but with a passion for philately. (which started as a mere hobby) He built a brilliant career out of it. In fact, he was a pioneer in his field inventing first day covers with special cancellations. Not only did his "willful independent" way pay off career wise, it was key to meeting challenges to come as well as embracing exactly what he wanted out of life... including his future wife, Hilda Gabriella Fisher, a Viennese girl he met while on a trip to Munich, Germany.

Hilda's side of my family was pure Austrian for generations. Of course, it intrigues me to learn of the commonalities between us though I never knew my Grandmother. The women of that family line were all singers, another gift from the Gods to be proud of. My great grandmother was an opera singer and Hilda as well. Aunt Billie became a cabaret singer and recording star in Brazil and went by the name Sandy Lee. And though I myself was unaware of this aspect of my lineage, I started my theatrical career as a singer as it happens. In fact, I had toyed with the idea of a career in opera. I studied over by Carnegie Hall with the wonderful Marion Proschowski whose husband had designed a special teaching methodology for opera singers. Yes, I was quite serious about this but in the end I went into theatre and musical theatre instead.

There's not much information about my Great Grandmother other than the fact that she married, had two girls, then divorced her husband during a time when it was a rarity to divorce. She then married again to a Catholic man by the name of Fisher who adopted the girls.

They were struck by a terrible tragedy when my Great Grandmother, at an all too young age had a massive stroke and was completely paralyzed. How the household was ever managed after that I can't begin to imagine. I suspect it created great unhappiness because according to Billie, Hilda and her mother never got along after that. She and her sister actually left the home as a result when she was just a teenager at 16. This was around the time my Grandparents met and fell in love.

What I was able to gather from the recording was that while on a business trip to Germany, Sam met Hilda the evening he'd gone to the theatre where she was apparently performing. You see, when she and her sister left home, they signed with a prestigious and well-known light opera company in Munich.

I wish we all knew more of the actual meeting between our Grandparents. But I can almost imagine my dapper grandfather sending flowers or at the very least a love letter backstage to Hilda, because evidently their romance blossomed quickly after that. Sam proposed, Hilda accepted and he literally bought out her contract for $20,000 Deutschmarks so that they could be wed. They left for Vienna where he was prepared to settle despite whatever anyone had to say. And apparently many had much to say. The story, of what followed always amused me (it was clearly not so amusing at the time for my Grandfather, however). Upon hearing the news that Sam had met an opera singer, had proposed, and was leaving Romania to marry her, the brother, Yoji came to Vienna to talk him out of it. For one thing, you understand, "entertainers" in those days were considered lowlifes! Yoji came on behalf of the entire family so you can imagine how serious they considered the situation. There was no talking Sam out of marrying Hilda however. The story goes that my Papa Sam got so furious with his brother that he took a plate of food and threw it at his head!. And that was the end of that.

I suppose one could say the Bayers were "passionate" folks that didn't hold back on their emotions, to say the least. In any event, my grandparents did marry and remained in Vienna for a few years... Their first child Billie, was born in 1922. My mother, Madeline was born in Vienna a year and a half later (July 28, 1924) and shortly thereafter they moved to Milan. There, Billie had a profound experience that obviously impacted her life. Frankly I found the story to be comparable to some of my experiences that I think of as mystical. Whether one wakes from a dream or vision, the psychic power of such experiences can be very meaningful, maybe archetypal actually even to a 3-year-old. So, Billie described such a vision. She and my mother who was all of 2 and Billie 3½, shared a small bedroom in their Milan apartment. In her words," I woke up and saw the statue of a saint suspended over Mady's crib. The two of them floated in the air together and I started to scream because the saint was taking Mady away. I screamed and screamed. This vision never left me." Of course, she told the mother the story. And some years later Hilda referred to the vision along with the statement that the girls had actually both wanted to be Catholic and so were sent to school in a convent. As I listened to this, I had to take pause because my own memory brought up a similar childhood sentiment. When I was just a girl… I'm going to guess this was around 2nd or 3rd grade, I came home with a Christian cross a friend had given me. It was of Jesus of course and I must have found it to be so compelling that I informed my mother and stepfather that I was going to reform. Incredible! When my parents denied me… no, shamed me, I remember becoming hysterical. I don't know where these archetypal energies come from but they are very real, very powerful, and very much an integral part of our psyches… But to have found out years later of my mother's feelings, indeed makes me want to soul search the subject. There's more to this in my life for sure and I will explain later. Returning to Billie's story, I found it interesting that Saints, Catholicism, and convents may very well have comforted her. But the statement about being Jewish really intrigued me. "I knew I was Jewish," she said, "but I was Italian first!" Interesting, yes? I hold no conclusions but wonder if persecuted Jews sometimes picked up on the mass prejudice against them and either bought into it or unconsciously wanted to deny their Nationality… Something like this. I don't know. When it comes to defining one's identity it's not always easy to take pride when the world is against you. It takes courage to be fully oneself anyway. Isn't that what the journey is about in the end? I will tell you this however, when it comes to my nationality, I am proud to be Jewish and relate on many levels to this great part of me but in the end, I am multitudes! And therein lies more the notion of my identity.

The family moved to Rome because Sam knew his philately business had a better chance near the Vatican (which it did). In Rome, Guido Bayer, my Uncle Guy was born in 1930. Now this intrigues me as I remember my mother telling me how she and Guy played as kids in the woods. They must have been on the outskirts of Rome for this to have been true. Even though their place was called a villa it couldn't have been in Rome's center. She told me of a time she and Guy were playing in the woods and Guy was bitten by a snake, and Mady, bare foot as always carried him on her shoulder all the way home. When Aunt Billie spoke of young Mady, I took pause thinking that she might as well have been talking about me. Always in the woods... always wild and filthy. In my aunt's words, "If you wanted to find Mady all you had to do was look in the nearest tree." My God, how DNA can show up generation after generation! That was me. That was me and still is the sentiment I hold as a 68-year-old woman. Give me Gaia! And get me back to "the Garden". Well, get us all back to the Garden. We've come so far away.

The other statement Billie made about my mother was surprising as well but once again, revealed a hand-me-down trait I had never known about. My mother, according to Billie was "a true loner".

Life was good in Rome, at least for a good while. Sam by now was well known in his field. And it seems that stamp collecting was such a popular hobby back then that all sorts knew and befriended him including the likes of Mussolini himself. There are a couple of stories surrounding their relationship. Apparently, Mussolini wanted to build a bridge across from the monolith as a mark of power; a purely competitive venture as bridges were evidently built as a symbol of leaders' "prowess". He needed the perfect land to do so obviously and he saw it in my grandfather's land and so he tried to cut a deal with Sam. Well, of course this was the family home they'd worked to perfect and naturally had no intention of leaving. But Mussolini insisted. When he asked how much Sam would take for the land Sam said, "55 million lyres". And Mussolini said," I'll give you 5. Take it or leave it because if you don't the government will claim it and that will be that!" I couldn't quite tell what the actual upshot was to the building of that bridge but what I do know, was that shortly thereafter, they did leave their home and went to France, or shall I say, they fled. They were actually encouraged to go by Mussolini himself, and not because of his want of the land but, because of his concern for their wellbeing. As far as I could make out from the recordings, Mussolini who was more than aware of the changing "climate" in Italy, knew it was no longer safe for Jews. It seems that despite the obvious truth that Hitler was an ally, and that Nazism may very well have been inspired by Fascism, Mussolini was quite clear that anti-Semitism was no part of the Fascist ideology. It is said that Hitler loved Mussolini, but Mussolini hated Hitler. Thank God for favors that turn out to be life-savers! Who would ever have thought we'd have the likes of a Mussolini to thank along the way to our family's freedom!

Anyway, Sam was urged to move everyone to France before it was too late, and that meant as soon as possible. Within 2 months they resettled in Paris. They took what they could, managing some furniture, some rolled up canvases, jewelry etc.

In France their 4th child Eleonore was born. She was just a baby when things became hostile there. So, once again they were forced to move on. This suited Billie just fine as she'd never much liked France, whereas my mother had grown attached. In any event there was little arguing with fate when the time had come. They'd been warned by many in Versailles… a place apparently safe for refugees… but the final decision was made out of an act of survival and they left as quickly as they could the day after the bombing of Paris. One doesn't easily imagine the danger and panic of such times unless depicted in a film, I suppose. But Billie described the state of affairs in Europe in a way that brought a little reality to my naïve world view. Most Americans are indeed naïve.

So, they knew the moment was now. "Paris was Burning", and literally, the air was toxic. No one could go out on the streets without gas masks, in fact, and the Romanian consulate apparently had no more. They were lucky enough to purchase one for each family member at 360 francs a piece, from the Czech consulate. The story goes that my mother disappeared that day, I imagine in a state of despair knowing she once again was being forced to leave her home. Of course, we know what might have happened to her had she not been found. And it was Billie who went searching for her and as she put it, "threw her in a taxi and met back up with the family". With each move, they were forced to leave more and more precious valuables behind but once again with rolled canvases, the coats on their backs (their furs were considered precious in those days) and jewelry. When they got to the French border, guards with guns emptied their cameras and stripped them down naked before allowing them to cross the border into Spain. From there, by the skin of their teeth they made their way to the Spanish frontier and transferred via ship to Lisbon, Portugal. Billie's description of their journey was quite hard for me to decipher, to be honest. I can't quite tell how Sam held on to any of his merchandise but then again, he was evidently resourceful. The way in which they smuggled money across the French border seems unfathomable yet apparently the truth of what it took to successfully survive. Sam had gone to a chemist friend, who rolled up as much cash as possible into toothpaste tubes and the family members literally hid them in their private parts! (extraordinary)

They lived safely in Portugal while contemplating their next move, which was to immigrate to the US. They lived there in Hotels, pensions, and at last in a villa all the while planning an exit strategy (as so many others were as well). They tried several times to acquire visitor's visas but the tickets were bought up at the last minute by others who were more aggressive and possibly had larger pocket books with which to bribe. They remained there for 9 months and finally, with the help a cousin in the states by the name of Sylvia Lehrman, they managed the trip. It's quite likely they might not have been able to immigrate without her help. Much needed to be put into place. On Sam's side, he needed to prove his future worth as an honorable American businessman and citizen. And affidavits were demanded stating so. A fair amount of cash was demanded to the tune of $2,000.00 and a sponsor would need to "contribute" a minimum of $10,000.00. Sylvia was the one who found that sponsor. She was the head buyer for Maidenform bras in the US (according to another source she was an original designer). In any event, she got a Mr. Solomon, who also worked with Maidenform, to sign on for the Bayers and they were in luck, thank God. It's amusing to realize that we have the maker of women's braziers to thank for all of our lives, past, present, and future! Thank God, yes and thank you, Maidenform! Fortunately, in the end Mr. Solomon never had to pay the $10,000.00 fee. But Sam was apparently on his third $2,000.00 payment towards a visa that would hold out long enough for the family to board and finally move on to America. The Consulate had shut down on and off for a while, I suppose as a result of the chaos at hand and I can only imagine how stressful the situation was by now. But Sam waited with a watchful eye and as soon as the doors reopened, he ran over, obtained the visa and now had to have the family go through yet another round of vaccinations.

It seemed all had been taken care of and they'd be on their way once securing tickets when one more drama struck. While closing up the household, the maid (who Billie in no uncertain terms labeled outrageously stupid). Yes, the maid who'd been ironing for some unknown reason, stood the piping hot iron on the floor and Eleonore who was a small toddler fell on top of it and got severely burned. If this wasn't serious enough this maid proceeded to wash the baby down with laundry detergent! This was all of two days before their departure and they really didn't know if it was appropriate to leave given the trauma the baby had suffered. They sent for a doctor who gave the go-ahead, knowing a physician would be on board and that their visa would not last any longer. They wrapped young Eleonore and boarded the "Loretsa Marcus" on her first voyage... but the last liner to bring refugees to the United States. They arrived in America on January 28th, 1941... Finally, they were truly on the way and Freedom was just ahead.

The voyage however, according to my Aunt Billie was treacherous. They were put in the 3rd class section which was apparently terribly overcrowded and set up with bunkbeds. They were immobilized the first two days because of a typhoon. The only one in the family who didn't get sick was Billie, while women all over the ship were literally having heart attacks. Somehow midway they were lucky enough to get permission to transfer (mattresses and all) to another area of the ship called the smoking quarters. Better than nothing. This permission came from the captain because resourceful Sam had with him a letter of recommendation but from whom? We'll never know.

In any event, they lived through it all and landed on American soil February 8th, 1941; a cold day to be sure. But I can only imagine what it felt like to have finally arrived in their new home; their new country!

Of course, no one spoke a word of English except for the little that Sam knew. But somehow, they managed and I'm sure there was such relief to be on safe ground, that the early hardships were looked upon as a great adventure. Cousin Sylvia set them up for a while and they moved around from Hotels to apartments. And with the help of Joe and Helen Roth, Sylvia's first cousins, they made their way with small jobs till they got their footing.

Mady finished High school quickly, learning the language which was merely one of several (This seemed to be the way of the Europeans who were facile when it came to language from the beginning). My mother studied art and I was lucky enough to acquire some of her original drawings. She was quite an artist... always was... Both sisters however, got their first jobs at Gimbel's where Billie worked at the Revlon counter and my mother worked as a model for Chanel robes. It didn't hurt to be a beauty with a charming French accent. She was a great success making $18.00 a week. She was 17 years old.

There at Gimbel's, destiny would take one step further when she left work one day and encountered a young sports clothes salesman in the Gimbel's elevator by the name of Clyde Sarzin (or shall I say when he encountered her!). The story indicates that it took time for him to approach her but he fell head over heels and did his best to pursue her. My father was a very gregarious fellow with more charisma than most. But in his own way he was apparently shy when it came to my mother and so had his love letters delivered to her by his good buddy. According to Billie, my mother never felt truly loved or given enough attention to growing up and so Clyde's attentiveness was much needed. Their love affair was true blue and they married 11 months later on August 30th, 1942. And though their marriage did not last a lifetime together they loved each other madly (at least for a good long while). Billie spoke of the fact that Mady was so in love that she was actually afraid to share that love with children. Of course, she was practically a girl herself but according to Billie, my mother needed to be loved and wanted as she'd never been before. I'd never known about this. How would I have as I was so very young when she died and I never really questioned her love for me. But now as I look back with this perspective, certain things and behaviors fall into place.

In any event, after my parents married, Billie met her first husband, and American life for them all continued to grow with a sense of renewal and freedom. As far as my grandparents were concerned, they had bought a home in the country but sold it early on and settled in Manhattan because of Hilda's heart troubles. I'm skipping over a number of years without too many specifics to speak of, but this does stand out. Hilda, like so many women in my family line, was taken by heart disease. And I can only imagine what it must have been like for the youngest, Elly, when her mother died in her arms of a heart attack. Death be not proud. They'd made it through the turmoil of wartime to leave their home in Europe and find a new one here in "The land of the free". But fate and destiny are forever bound together and sad as it is, we can't escape the inevitable.

I can tell you this, my Grandfather lived a good long life and had one more child, Daniel, with his second wife Mado, who became one of the most beloved people in my life. To her, "I was the daughter she never had" and to me, she was my Anam Cara grandmother and one that never needed to be blood kin... For she was a soul kin.

I am sorry to say I have very little information about my father's people. I have more by way of impressions and a few memories of how my father spoke of what we jokingly would call "the olden days", a phrase I used with him as a little girl after the divorce if I was feeling somewhat nostalgic for the days when we were still together. I remember sitting on his lap asking for him to "tell me again about the olden days." That warmth we shared lasted for only awhile. It seemed to vanish after my mother died when I returned to his household and a family. I'd have to get to know them having been separated from my sister for at least 7 years. And Clyde then remarried and adopted a young boy I'd soon come to know as my stepbrother Evan. The timing of all this will be made clearer, once again from excerpts written some years ago.

What I recall learning about the Sarzins however, is that unlike the Bayer's, these folks had been in America for some time. And I know little of my great grandparents. My ancestors apparently came from Portugal and Russia. When they came to this country, I simply don't know but that my father, Clyde and his sister, Jeanette grew up in Brooklyn NY with his mother Edith and father Bernard (who incidentally died of a heart attack in his forties). And as a result, my father went to work at a very young age to support his family.

He never went to college as his responsibilities were too high. But he nonetheless became a self-made man. Eventually he learned the stamp business from Papa Sam and became very successful.

I can't say I had the greatest relationship with Clyde. I don't really believe we had a chance beyond my early childhood as I was no doubt too deeply in a state of mourning to possibly have connected to him at the time... He was really very different than me in so many ways that I felt overwhelmed by his manner. Yes, he was charismatic but perhaps too extroverted to truly "see me" when it was my soul that craved a soul-to-soul connection. It wasn't meant to be except now and then when we spent time sailing or eating Japanese food before it became popular in America. I did enjoy hearing his tales of the olden days though; the ones about his youth and how much a hot dog cost or a ticket to the movies etc. Having already found the arts at that young age (which undeniably saved my life because it did touch my soul). Having found the arts, I was romanced by the story of his cousins who were vaudevillian performers. And here is where I have to say that despite our differences, there was one uncanny trait that we did share, and no doubt ran through the Sarzin bloodline that I'm so pleased to say he passed on. This may sound strange to you but there it is. The trait is a certain eccentricity that I like to think I took the best of. Perhaps it was actually the best of the Sarzins and possibly at times, the worst. But we are most certainly unique as a result. I suspect it only added to my sense of creativity and creative thinking and to be honest, a kind of spontaneity that has always helped me lo the many years of my life. Yes, my father passed that gift down to me even though it so often channeled through his life in ways that didn't serve him or others. Then again, whether we got along or not, I know he had his own valid journey and what I did love about him was his zest for life.

My father didn't do too well with his love affairs I'm sorry to say. He married 4 times and fell in and out of depressions despite his almost manic way of being in the world. He was much too much a drinker (actually diagnosed an emotional alcoholic), and finally died of cancer at the age of 72.

You know, I always wanted a closer relationship with him, but I had a different need than what was ever available within him to give and he knew it. For that I feel sorry. But maybe an introvert and an extrovert don't necessarily blend easily in the end. I do miss our days sailing the Long Island sound however. And there are days I miss his wild nature… as overwhelming as he could be.

2

REFLECTIONS: TIME REMEMBERED

Some years ago, before lifetime chronicles or even poetry, I began writing a collection of performance art pieces called, "The Traveling Fool". They were part of a larger work in progress inspired by my love of Carl Jung's Archetypes and the Tarot. The Fool begins the Heroine's journey, in a sense representing the "everyman" within Humanity. And every archetype, in the Major Arcana represents an aspect within and without. The philosophy of the Tarot suggests of course that we have a world of inner aspects... In fact, we are multitudes. And if we are able to coalesce and allow the all that we are, to collaborate, then The Fool indeed becomes the wise Fool. This is the hope of any man's journey; to become whole... To bring one's many inner voices together as a working team.

I think the truth is, we are all of us mythically vast containing multitudes, as described in my all-time favorite quote by Walt Whitman. One's identity is expansive, to say the least despite our uniqueness. And in these recent times of "spiritual awakenings" many are becoming increasingly conscious of that very fact.

Perhaps in my case, the sentiment went hand in hand with my early inklings of eternity, infinity and with multitudes in every way, shape or form. At first, we come in barely conscious but the wisdom of the ages is there within us and it reemerges through time in various ways through our symbols, dreams, through our bliss, our destiny, and even through our fates. We are multitudes within a holographic Universe and this inkling was wired into me from the beginning.

Most little girls play with dolls. I'd rather play as a wild child in the woods or spend time in apparent mystical meditation hooked to the creative unconscious. I was no more than 3 when I already was experiencing most unique visions. I would sit cross legged before the tall picture windows of our home that looked high above the tree tops, musing upon clouds, and building grand mythic creatures and Gods and Goddesses. Dolls had nothing over my visions; particularly the one I'll recall to my dying day as it could never have come from a 3-year old's mind had its imagery not been truly ancient, universal, and left symbolically on the sands of time in this little girl's mind. They say mathematics is the language of the Universe... Well, this was my uncanny vision:

I am in Egypt. There are pyramids all around... a blazing sun sits high in the sky. And as with other visions, I saw, as if through the lens of a moving camera, an inverted pyramid with an endless series of numbers and mathematical equations expanding through the sky and beyond... reaching out into the cosmos... all the way into infinity.

I must have been an odd little girl to have been drawn to abstract notions such as infinity, eternity, time and timelessness. Or perhaps not. Perhaps the nature of the cosmos is known somewhere inside us till we forget. But quantum physics suggests the history of the world and perhaps even the future are forever present. My obsession with it all began as a 3-year-old. I was so young but already open to oh so much I later studied or as they say, downloaded.

Anyway, I was evidently born a little spiritual being with a love of "the mystery". And that love has never left me. It simply developed through my experiences. But it seems clear this was coded within me from the start. Like fractal waves of my own secret destiny, everything brought me to the larger quantum world. My early "knowing" or taste for the greater shebang became the gestalt of my mystical life. Naturally it came with an appetite to know more, to expand, to inspire expansion in others, and to use the all that is within and without as an artist.

THE EARLY YEARS

"In a land far far away lived pixies, and elves, and goblins.
A fantasy which I had fallen in love with."
By Astald Elven

I was born in Roslyn, New York in the early fifties. My parents, Clyde and Madeline had already had their first child, Stefani, four years before. I have memories of that time though my family moved away when I was only two. I still have images of being in my crib calling out to my parents in my little voice: "Mommy, Daddy." I can see my little feet in Dr. Dentins. I see my sister's bedroom from the crib, and there is a warm morning glow through the window. I remember the dinner table right outside the kitchen hatch where my sister and I would flip peas off our spoons. I have fond memories of the two years I lived there. I remember sitting cross legged before the black and white TV mesmerized by "The Wizard of Oz". I remember the rooms, the architecture of the house, the colors of the walls, the 50's deco style... I remember an old banana that had fallen to the floor from my crib only to be covered with ants the next morning, crying over the sight and calling for help... I remember the sleigh rides down my backyard hill on Mommy's lap. And I remember being held in her arms.

The first two years of my life were warm and, for the most part, extremely loving and innocent. Now and then I suppose the seeds of my traumatic future revealed themselves in the works, but mostly I lived the early 50's life of hope and glory in the aftermath of war, and the bright American dream that the world admired and desired. There was a feeling of optimism and freedom in the air, at least within my family and in those parts of the States.

I think my father brought American hope into his entire world, along with his powerful zest for life. He had already overcome his poor Brooklyn upbringing when his father died and he had to support his mother and his sister when he was still a young teenager. He did so with verve and pride and never felt the sense of lack that hit many others in the Depression. No, my father was a man who seemed to be passionate about life and had an energy and style that was larger than life. An ingenious thinker, he claimed he could read a novel a day. He loved a good time – a wild party with fun-loving friends, good food, good booze, good everything. And eventually it became too much for everyone. But I'll say this... in the early years I remember the joy... the fun... the almost childlike connection we girls had with him... and with each other.

My sister was 4 years older than me and from what I remember, she was almost as charismatic as our father... certainly, as energetic. It's interesting to think that I was the one who became the actress and the performer when I never sought the spotlight in the early years. Perhaps it was my sister who originally taught me the way to abandonment on the stage. Back then I quietly absorbed my life and whenever I could, I watched from Mommy's arms. There's no doubt in my mind however, that ultimately my sister remains the extrovert and I, the introvert... or perhaps better said, the introvert/extrovert.

In any event, I was the quiet child and it intrigues me to this day that I became a boldly expressive individual and artist. And I can't say that I'm not without a certain charisma myself. I wonder sometimes however, if some children actually live in another state of consciousness for a while till the outer world demands linear focus. As I reflect, I can almost reenter the strange, innocent place I lived, and have to admit, it was a lucky thing my mother was attentive at the most vulnerable time of my life. I would have wandered ingenuously into all sorts of trouble, if she hadn't been there to protect me. I was just plain open... quiet, but open to it all.

I was the one she took when the breakup of the marriage occurred. Maybe she related to my quiet nature or simply felt I needed her more being the youngest of the two. I think subconsciously the decision to split us up between our parents left its mark. Naturally we've "worked it out" but on a deeper level, such events send forth fractals of fate and destiny. Innocence breaks apart bit by bit in the human heart and much happens to our character as the world enters in. And without the shadow's appearance in our life, we never really have a chance of living from the soul. Traumas large or small fill our memory boxes and partly shape us. I have come to understand that our wounds serve as the opening to our vulnerability in the world. And the themes may play themselves out over and over, initiating and reinitiating us towards our deepest purpose. Some, many, spend their lives running from early traumas, but I think we are given what we're meant to, or what we can handle. How we deal with it is what makes us talented alchemists or victims of our karma. I suspect when Hillman spoke of the soul's code, he most certainly took into account that perhaps our darkest experiences are part of that coding.

For the record, there were several "dramatic" events that I either witnessed or experienced that I don't care to speak of. But I will say this; I've had a lifetime of healing a whole lot of wounds and continue to honor and transform as best I can because of them... Beyond too many specifics, I knew there was trouble brewing in the family, and there were no doubt early signs of some emotional disorders that would reveal themselves later.

When I was about 2 years old, we moved to a beautiful home in Sands Point, just up the hill from the bay. I always refer to it fondly as "The House on Lighthouse Road". My sister and I would live there together with our parents for two more years. It was a stunning house and though I was taken from it when I was merely 4, I remember it well. I believe it became a part of me. I actually think one of the things that came to define the chapters of my life were various houses that I lived in. There were many. I even dreamt of houses of all sorts and sizes for years and years as they were evidently important symbols for me. And I came to understand them in Jungian terms sometime later. But this, the second house I lived in as a young child, clearly inspired my sense of beauty opening my awareness of the beauty in the world itself. I think the artist within me was born here. I am told my parents designed it... There was something about the atmosphere inside and out that appealed to me on a level that was obviously beyond my two-year-old sensibilities. Much like the architecture of a Frank Lloyd Wright, it seemed to live and breathe organically with vaulted ceilings and windows reaching to the sky, revealing the tall trees that surrounded us. I certainly never felt far from mother Nature... I hold many fond memories playing with my sister on that extraordinary property, not to mention just a short walk down the hill was our private strip of beach. My lasting impressions of the architecture and surrounding landscape seem as strong and meaningful to me as my relationships. And they somehow represent, spiritually... or energetically... the Home of my Soul...

So much beauty surrounded me during that time and, without a doubt, it had a profound effect, particularly because by now I was spending a good deal of time alone. My sister was in school and my mother and father made their own work hours. Though they were at home through much of the day, they slept into the late hours of the morning behind their locked bedroom door.

I suppose I should bring up the notion of Fate and Destiny again right around now. My core wounds no doubt began here with fractals galore... This was the first cut... Abandonment... It seemed that my every morning would end with hysteria and despair. Beating on my parents' door made no difference at all. They simply slept while I cried in the most primal of ways day after day for God knows how long. This ritual lasted until some semblance of a survival instinct kicked in, and I would find some way to find solace in my time alone... while my parents slept their days away because of the barbiturates they'd become addicted to... and a lifestyle that destroyed their marriage and their minds.

I feel for the child within who suffered abandonment issues and who no doubt felt the madness of her parent's marriage. But I'll say this again... We come into the world with spiritual issues and if we can imagine that everything that happens to us has meaning and purpose, then finally we begin to see the design of our own soul. Abandonment would involve some kind of karmic patterning through my life, but it was as if I was destined each step of the way, to go inward as a result... inward to find my own creative resources that only I could have found myself... inward to the stuff of spirit and soul, and into the psychic realm of the creative unconscious... inward towards imagination and to feelings, all sorts of feelings that would have to be tended through my life. The Wound is the way in...

We're all the same in that our life's spiral begins here. Is it all arbitrary, or is it all part of the making of character and purpose? The artist and the soulful seeker were born in this house.

And therein lies the story of a destiny fueled by fate.

We always had cats. I look back on my life and I can't recall living without at least one cat even when I did national tours in my early 20's. I've had so many cats... my constant companions. When my sister and I still lived together we had a few. I recall Busybody and Busby and a litter of kittens who remain the innocent cast of characters present the day my parents broke up.

I didn't often play with dolls, though I remember doll clothing we evidently collected for a few Genie dolls (the 50's version, I suppose, of Barbie). The Genies meant little to me but they provided quite a wonderful wardrobe for the kittens (poor things). I recall the final hour of my stay in the Sands Point home was spent dressing them in the vestibule by our front door. Everything could be seen of the great outdoors from every angle of our house, but from the vestibule windows, on that final day, while dressing the kittens, the breakup of our parents' marriage played out like a drama on the driveway of our house. There had been fights before, many with lamps shattered against walls, and worse. But this was the end and we knew it. The final battle on the driveway became wild while chaos broke loose inside between all involved including those poor little cats... To this day I feel a certain guilt over the torture they had to bear though I'm sure they lived their lives without the kind of trauma we were left with. Anyway, by the time my mother came inside to whisk me away, hysteria had taken us all.

The next thing I knew, without preparation of any sort we sped away to where I couldn't even begin to imagine. I think I must have been in some kind of shock, but it seemed my life was to present a series of shocking experiences. And oh, so many would wind up in endings of life as I knew it. This became a pattern. My goodness, no wonder I became an actress. I was primed for the drama! And when I consider it, I suspect I came to feel at home in the spotlight of true dramatic theatricals when perhaps all I was really trying to do was find my soul and connect to a world around me that had always left me in a state of abandonment. Honestly, I so often found myself quietly observing the chaos around me, perhaps hiding within myself while feeling somewhat paralyzed in the presence of so many crises.

But here's what's interesting… at least to me. Children find ways to buffer their blows and perhaps even find their medicine albeit sometimes in strange ways. I once again can say I found it in my soul's ability to connect with Beauty, and Beauty was almost always the priority.

And so, my mother took me and Stefi stayed in that big, beautiful home with our father. For a while we lived in my mother's art studio and it became my new home while everyone processed the crisis that had overtaken them. I was there during that transition in her life and though I can't say I was privy to the whole story of their breakup at the time, I can tell you this; I saw this sad and disturbed woman who was my mother throw her soul into her art. I think she was saved, at least for a while, by her prolific and remarkably beautiful creations. Mady was a magnificent artist who came out of the cubist movement. And I lived inside that studio amongst beauty and tragedy all at once.

I feel compelled to tell of my personal experience there as it remains one of the most powerful in my life. And though it took place amidst a terrible trauma, as an adult, I'm struck by the certain glimpse into… the Mystery perhaps… I'm not quite certain.

So, it may be hard to fathom, but I recall being left alone there, no doubt far too often, since once is already too much. My more mature self finds it unimaginable but it's true… and amazingly somehow, I got through. I may be entirely wrong but I tend to think that on some level I was eventually mesmerized by the art that literally surrounded me in an oddly perfect environment for a baby artist and soul searcher like me.

I recall waking in my little cot and though I must have been terrified to have been left at all, the feeling of abandonment completely escapes me. I see the studio in my mind's eye as if it was yesterday though I was really so small a child at 4 years of age. The experience of the environment, at least for a while trumped my loneliness. But as is the way of many artist types, I was already by nature somewhat of an introvert who enjoyed some solitude, because it offered soul time. Oh yes, I've always been one to vacillate between loneliness, and the peace, breath, and depth of my own interior life. Perhaps that's actually how I was able to navigate the difficult times my childhood presented. In any event, somehow despite the odds, I remember my time living in that art studio with great reverence particularly because of my relationship to my mother's paintings which were obviously influenced by the Cubist form of the times.

I guess I didn't have to be a mature intellectual to absorb the symbolic value of that style… To feel it and receive it was all that was needed. There must have been some pre cognitive recognition that went beyond maturity.

What I didn't know in a cerebral sense then however, is that art engages and speaks a language of its own… perhaps the language of the soul. And as far as I know, the more eternal part of that little girl was indeed in some soul-to-soul communication.

Cubism was probably one of the most potent art forms of all time, and at 4 years old, I was surrounded by it. In a sense I became a child of Cubism and am still drawn to it… to Picasso and his like… and of course, to my mother's few paintings that were left to us when she died. If ever there was an artful statement of that Holographic world of multitudes and the fractals within and without, it expressed itself through Cubism.

To this day, I feel Cubism made a firm impact on my world view, which consciously developed through my life. I absolutely love how it's described in Webster's: An early twentieth Century style and movement in art, especially painting, in which perspective with a single viewpoint was abandoned and use was made of simple geometric shapes, interlocking planes, and later collage.

In any event, good art brings the viewer and the maker into aesthetic ecstasy when all is said and done. And there is little doubt that my heart had already been broken with the breakdown of my parents' marriage, my mother's breakdown, and of course the family breakdown. Art, clearly became a metaphysical entry point to my psyche and soul's healing. And the abstract nature of Cubism particularly planted early seeds to the artist, the philosopher, and the lover of psychology… and of course so much more. Indeed, my way is a little like the story of "The Life of Pi".

I almost remember the smell of the oil paint in my mother's studio and how I grew to love it. How could I know the uniqueness of my life? These events were mine; the impressions were mine. A life is built upon some things universal and some unique. We know what we know until the blanks are sketched in by stories told by others. All I know is that one day my mother was taken from me, I was taken from her art studio, but an artful life had just begun and would remain my center forever more.

WEST END AVENUE

*"I've learned that people will forget what you said, people will forget what
you did, but people will never forget how you made them feel."*
Maya Angelou

Life had certainly become a whirlwind with regards to family and
roots by now. And it was apparently time to move once again, this
time to the West End Avenue apartment in Manhattan that belonged
to Papa Sam, his new wife, Mado, and her son, George.

I remember how taken I was with my elderly Grandfather. He
spoke with a thick Romanian accent most people really couldn't quite
decipher, but he was mesmerizing to me. He was the ultimate gentleman and perhaps in all my years, I've never met another that measured
up to his sophistication, with the exception of Uncle Guy, Papa Sam's
son, my mother's brother. Then again, these were Europeans from
another time and culture. I know much of my influence actually came
from them as they took me in after the art studio. I rarely saw my
mother or my father for that matter and was never told why until
sometime later. Apparently, my grandparents fought to keep me
despite my fathers' determination in the court of law. I'll never know
how they won. But there I lived on West End Ave till my mother came
for me much later.

The Sands Point house was sold. I don't know when. But the
picture of my family had actually grown dim through time, while I
slipped into this new world with its very different cast of characters.
Despite feeling misplaced and missing the warmth of my mother's
arms, life went on. I was deposited into an entirely new world and had
to adjust in some way, and I suppose I did, but not without a good
deal of acting out. The innocent child that I was, now began to show

signs of deviance, or at least shadow aspects that couldn't help but emerge. Though I came to love them all, there was no denying I'd been so obviously abandoned, and I would obviously respond darkly to my circumstances in some form.

And then there was the fact that I'd only known the country and very much missed that environment. The city was no place for a little girl like me. I remember feeling a bit like a caged animal, and would sneak out to spend time by the river (of course, an outlandish thing for a five-year-old to do). But the water called to me. It still does. In fact, when my mother died and I was brought back to my father years later, I would spend hours every day on the shoreline breathing in the ocean, my oldest friend, and perhaps my closest link to God herself. This little five-year-old who wandered down to the riverside in New York City needed her mother, and probably needed that link to God that the water might offer, but instead I was beaten for my deviant behavior. And then, the wooden spoon was made known to me for the multitude of crimes that I would commit from then on.

I was a curious child still open to the natural world, but openness and the sort of confusion I'd been experiencing couldn't have been a worse combination. I suppose my initial feelings of being caged in precipitated other experiences as well. All I know is that one Spring day for some reason, I was struck by an open window in my Grand-father's apartment. And it called to me... just like the river had called to me. And I followed some adventurous whim that I can't quite explain except to say that I can recall an incredible sense of freedom as I climbed out, and sat my little self-down on the air conditioner jutting into open air, 14 stories over Manhattan. I was free. I can remember that feeling. It was as if I had transcended my predicament and could just take off like a bird or a spirit with wings! But of course, my joy would not last for long. Like a pattern already set-in stone, my joy would turn to hysteria. I have Mado to thank for my life, I suppose. I might have fallen to my death. But all I knew was that freedom and peace were shockingly yanked from me when they yanked me back into the apartment and I got the beating of my life. I don't know what happened to me; I became a wild child. I continued to act out mostly through stealing and sometimes through lying, though I rarely lied actually. It made me feel queasy inside, and I guess what I really wanted to do was express my growing desperation, but simply couldn't.

I suspect, scattered as they were, the rest of my family had to have been working through their own heartache and confusion. Years later I heard that my father battled a version of a nervous breakdown, while my mother had actually been institutionalized. And that was why I never saw her that year. I'm sure my sister suffered too. Who gets away scot-free from life's wounds? I recently heard an interesting thought on the subject. The idea goes like this: It becomes increasingly important to stand on the actual ground of your sorrows and feel them... or they will haunt you forever more. And how do you know you're finally standing on that ground after so many years of suffering? You'll know you're on firm and solid soil because of the new horizon set before you...

In any event, through my childhood breakdown I nonetheless walked away from my time at West End Avenue with a wonderful impression of those two. I grew to love these grandparents. Papa Sam's stories of life in Europe fascinated me, and I think layered my own character with a history that clearly is a part of who I am. I loved hearing stories of my mother. It made me feel closer to her, even the stories that described her as an even wilder child than me. According to Papa Sam, they had to bring her to a convent in Italy for taming. And then at one point while the family was on the move (as they were much of the time during the war) my mother couldn't be found at the last minute because she had gone off with a young lover she had just met. This was my mother. She wanted to live in the spirit of freedom. And of course, I can relate. There is often a feeling of restlessness and the need to live life fully, to let the spirit free, to dance, to breathe, to feel passion. I know many of us, the Bayers and the Sarzins, even down to my son, have this need inside that comes up differently at different times – our greatest strength; our greatest weakness. But it seems to be the stuff that makes for a creative life if understood and channeled well.

Anyway, my mother was an extraordinary artist as were others in my family. Perhaps our passions found their perfect container in the arts. I certainly found my entire salvation there and some of my inclinations started at West End Avenue when the grandparents finally put away the wooden spoon and bought me a ballerina's outfit.

There are many ways to find your Freedom apparently, just as there are many ways to bow down and kiss the ground beneath you. Like a bird with wings, I found freedom in my little tutu. Oh, to dance, even in the confines of a living room in a Manhattan apartment. mother Nature had come to visit me again, only now I found her inside my heart. To feel once again that the light still exists and so does one's soul.

Time passed. Mado embraced me and I her. Through the years she remained my touchstone despite the fact that there was no blood relation. The bond went deep. She introduced me to the opera and to the ballet, and through these I learned to play again as a child must, despite the most devastating circumstances. And play I did with mythic theatricality in fact! Every day I would come home from school, change into costume and begin the day's performance. Not only did I dance, but soon I learned to sing. Dreams of flying over a Manhattan skyline no longer were necessary. I seemed to have found a way to transcend my troubles. If the artist had been born in Sands Point, the performer came to life here in Manhattan. By the end of my time with Mado and Papa Sam, I was inviting the neighbors' children to my grand puppet productions choreographed to classical greats such as Beethoven, Prokofiev and Shostakovich. This was a remarkable means of expression for that wild nature that I possessed. I'm almost certain my childhood friends thought I was quite crazy… Perhaps I was a little. But I tend to think that the alternative to the kind of "crazy" that creatives possess, can lead to the wrong kind of crazy!

Sometime by the end of my sixth year, I was told my mother would be coming home. No one could possibly imagine my excitement. She was to be with me the day after first grade ended. I could hardly bear it. My beautiful mother was finally coming for me… my mother, my Goddess. I'll never forget my white-haired teacher announcing that we had ten more days left of school. And, as hard as it was to contain myself, I figured, I'd lasted over a year without my parents. I would be patient and last a little longer… And so, I counted back the days for the greatest gift of all, my mother. The countdown began.

Each day the teacher would stand us up, and each day I would turn to my partner and I would say, "Nine more days till I see my mother," and then "Eight more days until I see my mother," and then seven, and then six, and then five, four, three, two. I thought I would die for day one… but day one would never come. Oh, certainly not because my mother would never return, but because my teacher had played a terrible and most unjust game with us. My joy turned to horror when on day one she announced that we would begin our countdown from ten again. From ten? From ten again? Oh my God, my heart sank into a darkness I'd never known. I couldn't fathom what had happened to day one. And even I, a child, knew that something outrageously unfair had taken place, and I would be no part of it.

This was an unbearable experience for me and I could not accept it. I couldn't! I had let everyone know the day I would be finished with school. Everyone... my Grandfather, Mado, George, and of course my beautiful mother. It was all arranged. I would be with my mother on the very next day and not a minute later as far as I was concerned. This was all that mattered. I could not put up with an unjust world any longer. Enough was enough! And so, like a warrior of the spirit, I stood tall with my righteous stance and did not return to school. Nor did I return the next day, or for ten days more. Instead, I waited for my mother's arrival as planned. And when I saw her, I ran into those arms so unforgettable to me, so profoundly warm and loving. At last, I was reunited with my Goddess, and the whole world just went away.

A long-ago sense of security seemed to return almost immediately. It felt like nothing could break it for me again. And yet... I admit I found it a bit unsettling that after our long separation she would bring a complete stranger to our reunion. I was told his name was Tal. He was a young man she apparently knew well, though I'd never seen him before. And you might imagine I worried I wouldn't get my much-needed private time with her as long as he was present. But of course, he stayed. I was told then and there that they were planning to marry. And this young man, this complete stranger by the name of Tal... who incidentally was thirteen years younger than my mother, was to become my stepfather... No, I never did get that precious private time I'd so longed for and expected. And the course of my life once again changed forever more.

In any event, there was a backstory I was too little to have been informed of. And like a number of puzzle pieces thrown into the mix of my life by several sources, I had to finally decipher the story many years later. And so, I shall share it with you now. Apparently, near the breakup of my parents' marriage, Mady would spend days, sometimes weeks away from Clyde. Their lifestyle had caused enough chaos. Whatever issues she had with him, she finally realized were there to stay, and she could no longer tolerate it. Clyde later mentioned to me how she spoke so often of needing her freedom. Well, I can draw my own conclusions, having known my father – she'd never had true freedom with him because Clyde was overwhelmingly controlling. I know Mady was his first love and three marriages more would never compare, but people can't help themselves. They come into relationships with a certain nature. My father swallowed people up. He took over my mother's life and it couldn't last like that because she herself was a force to be reckoned with. I can see the many ways that freedom had become her life's theme. Unfortunately, her freedom finally came by way of psychosis. What appeared to be a nervous breakdown was then recognized as manic depression. From what I pieced together, the mania struck and erased all feeling of guilt and responsibility to the children, or to the declining marriage. She fled. According to Eleonore, her younger sister, she had become a different person, and though many of the details are lost to all of us, what we knew was that she spent time between her art studio and young lovers that she had met at the beach. Apparently the one who fell madly in love despite apparent craziness was Tal. He was really just a kid I think, 19 or 20, because they married when he was only 21, she 33 I believe. Tal fell for her and stayed on the scene through the separation, the divorce and the hospitalization. And then later, when my mother recovered from her breakdown and was planning to move with me to France, it was Tal who lobbied for her to stay. They married and I grew up in America. I so often wonder, however, what life would have been like in France. It might have been good. I am drawn to so much of their culture – their food, their language their music. Isn't it interesting that I chose to become a Mime and toured with my favorite show of all time, "Jacques Brel is Alive and Well and Living in Paris." France might have played out well, but that's not the way it went. I grew up in America and life went on.

So, this was the scenario. And coming back now to the story of our reunion, this was the reason Mady returned to me with her young friend. For me at the time, his presence was a worrisome curiosity, but her presence was the world. Every day they came to visit me that first week. And my mother and Tal would take me out on the town in her new red Thunderbird. I never thought of school and actually erased from my mind that my classmates had not even completed their "ten more days." I had completed them. I was finished with school and, besides, with my mother nothing could go wrong. But of course, it did go wrong. I would be found out. When I look back, I marvel at the kind of conviction I gave myself to that experience. I fully believed that the unjust action of my teacher would right itself through my own actions. But there was no easy way out of this lesson. The next week there would be more heartache on the heels of Mommy's return, more acting out, more discipline, more lessons learned, and more joy turned to tears. I was found out and sent back to school, but might as well have been sent to a dungeon for my crime. It would have been easier to handle than facing my own family or my white-haired teacher. Naturally she'd never admit to her own responsibility in the matter. I'd have to endure the rest of those days with shame and punishment. But worse, I would lose my mother's trust, not to mention that I lost my own sense of trust in a fair and understanding world… Somewhere along the line, I would have to fight for that. To compound it all, right around that time, I'd been wrongfully accused of spending money that I had been given for lunch. I remember as if it was yesterday, that I had actually lost that money. But no one would believe me. I suppose it was too late for fairness. I'd never be heard. I was perceived as a thief, a liar and a troubled girl in need of discipline to straighten her out. And that job would be given to my future stepfather, Tal.

Here is the story of a terrible taming that I will take with me to the grave… Tal and my beautiful mother held me down as if wrangling a wild animal. And they hit me with a belt repeatedly. Even wild animals will be brought to submission – it's a survival instinct. I had to lie to save myself. I screamed out in complete despair that they were all right about me. I stole that money, yes. I was a bad girl. I was a bad, bad little girl. I'll never forget it. It was Mythic.

What came after was a kind of paralysis and quieting of my soul for a time. Perhaps to them I couldn't be trusted, but how was I to trust anyone after this? Life is simply not fair. I suppose we all learn this lesson, each in our own way. Some grow up and become alcoholics to numb the pain of an unfair world that they had so little control over. Some give up in little ways and some in large. Some build character and a fighting spirit standing for the rights of humanity. But it's really nothing new. We, all of us, live with this human dilemma and the defenses we build in response to it. As far as I can tell, the only way to our own human frailty is to remember to feed the soul and find our way to forgiveness and compassion.

The Buddhists say that we must cultivate compassion within ourselves. It does not come without mindfulness. And learning to live with each other peacefully and lovingly is no easy trick, when our innocence has come face-to-face with the nature of life itself. We are all made of the same stuff. We are all the shadow and the light. And like the rose whose bloom is magnificent, it's as magnificent as anything that ever was; it cannot exist without the thorn. We hurt and we are hurt. And the healing, if there is one to be had, begins with forgiveness. I have forgiven everyone, but perhaps I am still working on trust.

Mommy and Tal married. We moved to Sunnyside, Queens. My father married again as well, though I rarely saw him. Most of my memories of that time are of the many nightmares that plagued me. I suppose I'd found a way to hide in the light of day, only to have revealed at night my awful fear that wanted out somehow. My dreams were wild with tumultuous storms where houses would shake, or be set on fire and explode. I remember a vivid dream of drowning in an ocean squall with trash all around me and buildings that had blown into the sea, lighthouses and windmills alongside, all caught in the electric storm that obviously was my inner life force gone haywire.

These were the beginning of my house dreams I'd have through much of my life. They would all change in tone and architecture as I grew into my own. But the main theme of my dreams at that time were of cars. Sometimes I'd be in the passenger seat and no one would be in control of the car, yet the car would drive itself, and it was always quite terrifying. Even when I would try to take the wheel, I couldn't. I never knew how to drive the car, never.

In any event, these were obviously difficult, perhaps even traumatic times for me emotionally. I was disciplined constantly, though really, I never knew what for. By now I had quieted down so much that I couldn't imagine why I was so scrutinized for my every move and made to feel like I was indeed a very bad girl. Through all of this, however, my mother and I still carried on our love affair. Through thick and thin we would shower "I love yous" to each other and "I love you infinity times to the ends of the universe and back again." I know that love would be my tender through the tough times. And whatever infinity itself meant; I'd been having profound glimpses of it from very early on… I had entered into the bigger picture through my dreams and visions. And of course, to this day I return to the dream of my Egyptian pyramid and its endless series of numbers, expanding through the sky and beyond. I wondered for the longest time how abstract thought… or perhaps higher thought could crop into the undeveloped mind of a small child. Could it have been that my life's experience had brought me to another world or realm that happened to be surprisingly creative and almost cosmic in its nature? The vision was obviously beyond me, but perhaps the life that had taken me inward in response to difficult circumstances had brought me to a kind of portal, a gateway into what Carl Jung called "the creative unconscious." I became an artist with easy access to the collective mind. Perhaps this was the blessing of my journey (or the blessing of my fate). Life is indeed a mystery and though to some degree we learn to manipulate its course, perhaps the soul has a purpose of its own. I honestly believe everything happens for a reason and even the darkest experience may render tremendous value in one's life.

KATYKILL MOUNTAIN

"When despair for the world
grows in me
and I wake in the night
at the least sound
in fear of what my life
and my children's life may be,
I go and lie down where the wood drake
rests in his beauty on the water
and the great heron feeds.
I come into the peace of wild things
who do not tax their lives
with forethought of grief.
I come into the presence of still water.
And I feel above me the day-blind stars
waiting with their light.
For a time, I rest in the grace of the world,
and I am free.

By Wendell Berry

Some wounds never heal and need to be tended through one's life. My summer near Katykill Mountain in 1958, would leave me with such a wound. And, as I reflect upon it now, I realize that my terrible hunger to be loved made me the perfect victim for a pedophile.

It's truly horrifying to know how many there are of us, and worse to realize how often these offenses occur when loving parents with the best of intentions leave their children at such places as summer camps.

I know my mother needed to land in her new life and needed time with her new husband. And I'm sure they felt I deserved a country getaway... Summer camp would seem to be the perfect offering for everyone. I'd been to camp before and had many wonderful memories. I cherish so many, like chasing fireflies in the early evenings, like the costume pageants, the musicals, the dances, the horseback riding, and oh so many more. My summers away were filled with the pure joy of being in nature, something that to this day I simply cannot get enough of. Too bad the cruelty of sexual abuse had to mix amongst the many beautiful experiences that I'd had there.

Why, though, did it happen to me? Why indeed? Pedophilia is a strange affliction. I say affliction because I believe it is a compulsion of a sad and diseased soul. I didn't think it at the time but lo, these many years later when I think of that 21-year-old head counselor who had his way with me, I feel as sorry for him as I do for me. And oddly, I know he and I share a strange and peculiar bond of some sort that connects us to the many who have been abused and who abuse. What's it all about? Rage? Or is it about a profoundly wounded heart, so wounded that a crime brings persecutor and victim together.

I was not raped. I was seduced in a way that didn't take much cunning on his part, because I'd had such a weak, vulnerable heart, and I only wanted to be noticed. And not only did he notice me, he seemed to connect to me and appreciate me when most did not. My relationship to my persecutor was utterly mesmerizing. I honestly think that young man had put me into a trance that summer.

Otherwise, how could he have made me do the things that I did and allow him to have such deviant ways with me?

I rarely revisit that summer, but when I dare to, I clearly recall the strange and awful feeling that I experienced each time that I was alone with him, like being drugged or frozen in time. And yet I let him take control of me over and over and over again, till one day I spoke in my small, quivering little voice and asked him to stop. I just asked him to stop! With tears in my eyes, I told him to leave me alone. And, that easily, without a fuss, he agreed. He left me alone! But I felt punished somehow for ending it with him because I had lost his attention and I'd lost his love and worse, he didn't seem to care. How strange and sad was this experience for me. In the end I was left feeling so lonely and so violated that I could never tell a soul for years.

The following summer I was sent back against my will and I was relieved to find that he wasn't there, except for one day when I was called to the boys' bunk house. They said I had a visitor. I hoped it was my mother. But when I arrived, I found Ronnie sitting on the porch waiting for me. I froze. He looked a little older and had gained some weight, but I knew him alright. I remember how he sweetly called my name, "Erica, Erica, come on up here and visit with me for a while. Erica?" He called me repeatedly as I stood below like a deer who had encountered her killer. I think I'd have remained frozen to this day, but something within me fired up from God knows where and I found myself running like the wind with a speed I'd never known. I ran and I ran and ran and when I could no longer run, I hid in the woods until I could breathe again knowing he was gone... And I was certain that I'd never let myself be overtaken by another again. There was too, too much of that in my life already.

But something strikes me now when I think of all this. Of course, this is my personal story and I would not wish it upon my worst enemy. But there is always a Universal component to our stories and experiences. We may not all of us have experienced actual abuse, but we all do struggle to find and hold our sense of power, don't we? We all want some true autonomy, love and respect. To this day I feel anxiety rise up in me like a flood when I sense even the slightest bit of my power taken from me by another. And I will tell you this, having worked as a life coach for as long as I have, I have seen, up close and personally, that power is one of the foremost issues most people possess... If you were to ask me about this and how it fits into the grand scheme of the human condition, I would say this: We all of us have the right and the need to stay our ground and "be in our power". The problem as I see it, is that we either give it away, or engage in a power play by which we win or we lose... Where this inner struggle begins one never really knows but it seems nearly endless. It has affected women since the beginning of time, of course... but It's far more insidious than we like to think. They say every marriage gone wrong is due to power play as is every battle or war... The subplots within the Human dilemma are, existentially speaking, what we've come here to work through and they begin with the tangled threads of our personal fate and destiny... That was certainly the case with me. And as I return to these old pages from 11 years ago I can see clearly how certain aspects of my own character began to develop in response to all my experiences both "good" and "bad".

In the summer of 1958, I was all of 6 years old when I suffered the trauma of sexual abuse... This became a chapter in my story that would significantly shape me and serve as a most vital aspect of my destiny, despite or because of "fate"... And for that, believe it or not, I have a certain gratitude.

Oh, I would never speak of it to my parents or anyone, for that matter for years. One learns at a very young age to swallow shame and believe me, shame seems to always come with the territory of abuse... And as you may have surmised by now, I was already perceived as a problem child. To my mind this story no doubt would have been one more nail in the coffin. And so, I learned to hold much inside my own soul with secrecy (at least for a while). There were years of quiet, yet with so much to say. But I held it all inside till the time to express would come, and it would come like a flood. Until that time, I would disappear.

But then there is this: We find our ways to grapple, "get through" and live with all sorts of trauma. I almost think there is a kind of negotiation within our psyches when it comes to abuse, that allows parts of ourselves to live freely in the world while other parts get sacrificed or repressed... The ramifications of such wounding never truly disappear altogether. And there is no doubt, a tradeoff for the coping mechanisms one develops when trauma gets packed away. But when I look back to that summer by Katykill Mountain, what remains most potently in my consciousness is actually not my terrible trauma, but the beauty and the magic of that place and time. Of course, one could say that the "magic" was really of my own making, but I must admit, I found myself so taken by our mid-summer evenings chasing fireflies, that the reality of abuse seemed to slip away... Perhaps this was my childhood encounter with the Numinous, and with "Kairos time" as they say. But "Chasing Fireflies" became a lifetime metaphor of sorts for me; my little fable about the worth of "the eternal child" who in her inherent belief in Spirit could continuously tap into some greater truth and once again, beauty.

I turn again to James Hillman's notion of the Soul's code. I find the idea of this utterly compelling and will no doubt continue to delve into these memoirs from that angle as well as the initiations that brought me closer to the deepest parts of my being. Oh yes, we are multitudes, but there are primary characters who live in the light of our identity, I suppose. I'd already had a number of mystical visions and experiences but right around now, I believe the mystical within started to take the lead on many levels especially by way of imagination. Much of the time I daydreamed and yes, quite possibly as a coping mechanism... but what might have started out as a need to escape certainly eventually led to the gateway to so much more (so very much more).

Anyway, for now, I daydreamed. But what could I do? I just couldn't focus when my dreams were so much sweeter than reality. Although memories come to mind of sitting cross-legged inches away from my television set in utter awe of what America was witnessing at the time. I actually didn't have to look far for escape when the reality of our President's space program brought Jules Verne and HG Wells right into my very own living room! The whole idea captured my imagination in every way. And the concept of going to the moon was really not far-fetched, though I'm sure my fascination suggested a kind of romanticism despite or because of my troubles. Every night my mother would tuck me in by the window and we would say a prayer to the moon. I dreamed of time travel and traversing the cosmos itself!

I absolutely believed space travel would be made available to all of us in the not too far future.

Though by now I was still very young, I had already come to value a sort of personal collection of my life's bliss and personal array of symbols. Like pearls strung together, the symbols one is taken by may wind up partly defining his life, or at least enriching it. My symbols came by way of dreams and images of houses, oh so many houses, some on stilts deep in the forest, expanding houses, light houses, dollhouses, houses made of rich woods, and magnificently detailed mosaic temples. Then would come The Goddess dreams, tree dreams, ocean dreams, ships, sailboats, galloping horses, sea horses, pyramids, infinity, time travel and without any doubt, travel into the heart of the cosmos! I was a dreamer; a spiritually coded mystic in the making who was equally connected to Gaia. So much of what I dreamed of seemed to point the way to my soul, and the way of my soul at the same time.

Six years old turned into seven, and then eight. Sometime around fourth grade there was another move. Tal, Mady, and I moved to another redwood home in West Nyack, Rockland County, New York. Memories there were filled with the beauty of woods, and mostly, great times in nature. It seemed to appease something in me that always felt wild and untamed. I loved the forests and the trees. If I couldn't have the ocean, at least I could climb the trees. There was always the feeling of freedom in nature and the familiar sense of home somehow. I think there is an innate sense in many of us that is rekindled in the forests and the sea. Maybe it's our primal connection to our own natural origin. I felt it, but perhaps my life was shamanistic from the beginning anyway. One never really knows about these things, but certainly I knew that I came to life in nature's beauty, and I can almost imagine a tribal life, lifetimes ago.

Some normalcy set in for a few years in the Nyack house. I had friends and I played like a normal kid. I remember Christmas time in that house and the magical feeling it brought... a feeling I suppose I'm forever trying to reinvent. I remember gatherings at Mado and Papa Sam's and though I had been separated for so long from my father and sister, the sense of family had been re-ignited with my mother's people. I adored my Uncle Guy and my two cousins, Karen and Lisa. It was good. I could breathe again. There were people I could trust again and besides; I was growing up and starting to develop a sense of myself in the world. Even when I felt the proverbial rebelliousness of adolescence, my bliss led the way to music and art and a fascination with story and the morals that they would teach. I treasured my little golden books the way most girls treasured Barbie dolls. I still feel a little saddened that they, along with my other possessions, were given away to Salvation Army when I moved. But I really never had known about holding on to anything but my memories. The stuff of life had always disappeared with each move along with some of my roots, or so it seemed. This would happen again and again.

More memories of the Nyack house come up of the hours I spent sitting by our large living room window, staring at the clouds. This had become a daily routine actually, and interests me as I look back. I wonder if beyond the creative play of seeing pictures in the sky, I wasn't actually exercising a psychic mechanism. I do wonder because my psychic abilities would surface in a big way soon after. Simultaneous to this, my insatiable interest in existential matters started to emerge with my emerging consciousness. I wanted to know about life and death and the great creator. I asked my poor mother every question I could think of, and incessantly asked about God. We were Jewish, with a little Catholic background on my grandmother Hilda's side. But nothing in my family was actually practiced. Out of my hunger for knowledge, they sent me to Hebrew school for a while, but it didn't offer what I longed for possibly because I wanted more. I wanted to know God, I suppose, directly. I continued to plague my mother on the subject. I'm sure my obsession seemed almost obnoxious now that I think of it, because she finally put the kibosh on these conversations… and firmly redirected my search for spiritual truth… I'll never forget these words… They were profound… "Erica", she said, "God is within you. You will find Him one day. He is everywhere, but most importantly within." This answer stunned me; its concept was big, maybe as big as infinity. It was a perfect answer and perhaps, out of her frustration, she threw into my own young hands that the meaning of one's own life is found somewhere within. My journey I think was given a little meaning, a sense of purpose suddenly. I had to contemplate things now in a slightly different way, and I so thank my mother for giving that to me. It kind of made the mystery of life with all its hardships worth exploring, and that exploration has remained a vibrant one these many years later.

The Nyack times brought a spiritual consciousness to my world, and much was simply beautiful. But when I think back to those years, I also seem to recall my many childhood illnesses with high fevers. I can't say why they occurred, but apparently my immune system was weak. It seemed I was constantly sick and haunted by horrible delirium dreams. There was one about a perfect little scene gone into chaos, like Jacques Brel's song "Carousel". The song begins enchantingly but speeds up gradually into a ferocious cacophony of madness. He describes an orderly world of harmony and love and its opposite, which so often it becomes, a world out of balance and on the brink of insanity. I called that dream my dollhouse dream. It came with every fever and started and ended precisely the same way each time. The perfect, tiny, little, pristine dollhouse would explode as the furniture grew beyond its walls, expanding into chaos, and a dream that I would wake screaming from. These dreams were absolutely terrifying, but what a metaphor I've come to realize. And I have to say, they must have been clairvoyant in some way because the truth is the perfect little world I'd come to treasure in my Nyack house was soon to blow wide open, just like the dream of my dollhouse gone mad.

THE YEAR OF TRAGEDY

"We all leave childhood with wounds.
The injuries we have suffered invite us to assume
the most Human of all vocations... To heal ourselves and others."
Sam Keen

My eleventh year would bring heartbreak, and of the many memories I've packed away, these are the toughest to deal with to this day. I have to pause even now before telling the tale for fear of stirring up my old emotions... I'm speaking now of my mother's illness and death. Back then I seemed to find a way to cope; I'm sure most children who lose a parent early know the trick of living with a dying parent. We learn a way to keep smiling... even laughing, amidst crisis. And I who loved my mother through infinity and back again, found a way to get through it. And get through it I did, at least seemingly so. In the end, however, losing a mother, you so love, at such an early age may surpass and outlast the trauma of abuse.

I had another dream. This one came out of the blue before anyone suspected there was a problem, before symptoms and certainly before diagnosis. This was a psychic dream that would come to light in days to come.

> *In my dream I saw my mother standing in the dark. She just stood there as if against an abstracted backdrop, elegantly posed. I came closer, feeling almost like the lens of a camera that had the ability to scan its object. She stood in black quietly as I viewed her face and her head. She was beautiful as always, but my dream was emotionless till the very end. I was simply an observer. The camera went inside now to get a closer look, and this is what it saw. My mother's brain was infested. It looked to me like it was being eaten by parasites.*

The dream fell apart at that point. Suddenly I was no longer a cold, observing scanner, but my mother's little girl again. I remember waking up in a sweat and crying out for her in the night. It was a horrifying dream.

Soon after that, she started having terrible headaches. Why do I remember being at the doctors with her? I was so young. Could she have brought me into that examining room with her? I really can't fathom it, but I do remember her initial testing. What stays in my mind most was the doctor asking her how to spell the word "world" backwards. I don't remember if she answered correctly. That week she seemed sicker than ever and I recall my own anxiety and my concern for her.

The news came. She had a brain tumor. To the best of their ability, they explained what that meant. Several surgeries later my mother was no better. She was devastatingly ill. I saw her ravaged by illness through that year, and I have memories of ambulances arriving in the middle of the night. I'd sit by my window over the driveway as they'd wheel her out on a stretcher and take her away. This happened so many times, to this day I can't quite bear the sound of sirens and flash of lights. The visits to the hospital were constant. I'll never forget right after one of her surgeries, Tal unwrapped the bandages from her head to show me the stitches. Perhaps he thought the shock of it would set me straight because much of the time I was in denial.

There was a time I recall my mother cried out for me after one of her terrible hallucinations. She was convinced the Nazis had come for us and had surrounded the house. When it became clear there was no reasoning with her, I decided to play along. Often, I found myself in that position. I found I could calm her somewhat by playing into her delusion. I was eleven and a half by now and though I had predicted a devastating illness symbolized in my dream, I couldn't imagine she would die from it. I saw my beloved mother experience more suffering than anyone should ever know, and still I was in denial. What did I think — she'd go on forever like this? I don't know, but I couldn't let her go in my mind, even if it meant the end of suffering. I just couldn't. I loved her too much.

This was 1963. In the middle of this year so full of crisis came another, another crisis that affected the world. I remember it well. I was walking down the school corridor when I felt commotion all around, and then the word came out: President Kennedy had been shot and killed. Oh my God, what insanity! I remember the shock and the horror that we all felt. Our beloved president was killed, and it did personally affect us all, even children. Those were different times, to say the least. But somehow, they became part of my experience that year, bundled up with falling in love with the Beatles, my mother's illness, and growing into puberty. There was a lot to hold. But there you are.

School was to end soon now and honestly, I couldn't wait. I was more than ready for a vacation, perhaps a vacation from everything. I remember that Tal sat me down, I suppose once again for another serious talk about my mother. He must have thought that I was void of feeling because I certainly never showed any to him by this time. I swallowed everything while he was ravaged by tears and remorse. Something in me wouldn't reach out to him. I just needed to run away from it all and pretend that my Goddess would be well again. So, when the serious conversation came up this time, the only part of it I chose to respond to was that my father wanted to take me away for the summer. The rest of it was simply too painful to take in. I think I knew what he was trying to say to me. He was trying to say that she didn't have much time but I wouldn't hear of it. I couldn't. Of course, now when I look back, I feel a deep grief and the feeling of unresolved guilt because I could have chosen to stay with her. A loving daughter should have. Instead, survival mode took hold and my father had come to rescue me.

I saw my mother one more time before my father came for me. She'd been in the hospital and things by now had gotten pretty serious. The whole family gathered. Mado, Papa Sam, Uncle Guy, his wife Ina, and I squeezed into her hospital room and I remember having the strangest most uncomfortable feeling that they'd all been crying… or something. I remember the intense anxiety in the air, the kind you feel when something is horribly wrong. I was told to stay in the room while they went to talk privately but I froze. I just froze by her hospital bed not knowing what to do or say or how to be with her… with my beautiful mother.

And then she told me to leave the room. She told me that I needed to go to the others. I needed to go to my mother! She said, "Go to your mother. Why do you stay here?" Of course, I was more than confused. I was shocked. I'd played into her delusions before, but this one struck me through the heart. The tears welled up in me and I remember saying, "But… but you're my mother." "No!" she said, "Go to your mother! Go!" I couldn't believe what I was hearing. I cried out, "Mommy!" But she didn't know me anymore. She became increasingly disturbed by my presence and as devastating as this was, I had no choice but to leave her hospital room.

I left her and saw them gathered down the hall. I still see them. I tenuously started to walk towards them, knowing they'd be upset with me. As soon as Tal spotted me, he told me to get back into the room, that I shouldn't leave my mother alone like that... What was I thinking!!! I'll never forget the torment of the moment. I didn't know which way to go, literally. I stood in the middle of the hospital hallway choking on my tears. Eventually I went back, but there was a back-and-forth push and pull at least 2 more times till I thought I would scream. Of course, I didn't but something in me, despite my love for my mother, made me want to run, run like the wind, the way I did when I saw my old summer camp counselor. I wanted to run and hide from this terrible pain, but mostly from my conflicted feelings that I simply could not understand.

So, when my father wanted to take me away for the summer, I said yes. I said yes! And I didn't look behind because I'd convinced myself that she wouldn't die. I went off with my father who I hadn't been with for almost a decade, but that I pinned all my hopes on. So many divorced leave their children thinking there was a good guy and a bad guy, but I made no such judgment. I remembered his charm and his love of life, and I wanted that light of his more than anything. I needed him to be my hero. And so, I went with him and trusted that he would take care of every little thing.

With just one small suitcase I moved in for the summer to his home on Shorewood Drive, his second house in Sands Point. He'd been remarried now for a while, how long I'm not quite sure. I seem to want to say it was about six years, and I was welcomed by my sister, who was now 16-years-old. Though I had visits here and there through the years, we really didn't know each other. She was my older sister, however, and the reunion was heartfelt in some way, despite the fact that we were strangers in another. I always thought my father's wife, Helen, looked a little like Elizabeth Taylor. She was an astounding beauty with her black hair and cat eyes. I suspected she was better suited to my father than my mother had been... Certainly they were both party animals. The lifestyle everyone lived in this home was completely different from what I had known with my mother. And I can't say that I ever really fit in here, but it was a relief to be away from the incessant lecturing and discipline I'd grown up with, with Tal. And as you can imagine it was a greater relief to have a respite from illness and impending death. Or was it? I'm not really sure now when I look back. I was brought into a home now seemingly full of life. But in contrast to my sad experiences with my beloved mother, things seemed strange and peculiar here. I know my father wanted to protect me. But being back with this family wasn't quite the warm and cozy feeling I'd imagined. And my father never quite wound up my hero, though it was clear he had the right intentions. These things are never black and white, and life is really very much more complicated than one might assume. And though I did allow myself the right to truly enjoy my summer, I couldn't completely bury feelings of guilt or home-sickness for that matter.

I was a stranger on a vacation from the inevitable everyone was trying to overlook. It obviously came easier to my sister who had been living an entirely different life with entirely different family attachments than I. It came more easily to them all, as they hadn't truly been touched by my crisis. And Helen's son Evan who by now had bonded with my sister, was living with his own troubles and was far too young to be conscious of mine. In any event I did my best to get to know this other family, though mostly I felt on the outside looking in.

Despite all that was going on however, the great blessing of that summer and that which offered a kind of medicine, was the Sailing program my father had signed me up for. I loved every moment on the water. I always felt (and still do) that the ocean brings me into the Home of my Soul… somewhere beyond the present moment yet, into true presence. I felt a kind of joy and peace when I was on the water always perhaps because I knew I was with God at such times.

The summer program was a respite despite the rest of it. We went out every single day, and once we knew what we were doing, we'd sail regattas. Sometimes we'd skipper and sometimes we'd crew. I preferred to crew. Perhaps this was a throwback to my dreams of losing control at the wheel. I'd rather rely on others, at least for that time. I met my first real boyfriend that summer. And I must admit, even teenage puppy love will feel mythically romantic while sailing the seas, at least for a romantic like me.

He and I would sneak off together and find places to hug and kiss. We were really so innocent. It was a simple, sweet relationship that might have had a chance to live a bit longer, but ended abruptly when the tragedy came.

We had gone off to a two-week-long regatta in Larchmont, New York, and stayed with the kids from our sister yacht club. These were very wealthy kids who lived in mansions and every year would host teenagers from the Knickerbocker yacht club... The family I stayed with was wonderful as was their daughter... She was the perfect hostess... During the day we'd race our blue jays against each other. And in the evenings, we'd get together for club dinners, dances, or for the parties at my young friend's house that would inevitably end up in group make-out sessions. It seemed no one was without a boyfriend or a girlfriend. It was a great time for kids my age offering summer fun and summer love.

And then one day I had a most peculiar experience. We'd gone out sailing as usual, my boyfriend at the helm while I crewed. The day began no differently than any other. There was no summer squall or anything to have felt concerned about. The sail was going well until the wind died... which it's want to do at times... but this time it felt strange somehow... We sat for a while with the stillness and waited... and waited... And waited some more. I can't explain how or why, but a very bizarre feeling overtook me while we were suspended there in time. It was almost as if something from my subconscious came trickling in... In that moment of stillness on the water, for some reason I believe I went into an altered state... And though the "message" I received was not literal, I felt called to call home as soon as I could. And when I say home, I mean my home in Rockland County where I had left my mother who was dying while I was living, and not just living, but living it up.

I waited hours on that sailboat to come into dock and still longer to arrive at my hostess's home. Finally, I called. I spoke with Tal, though he couldn't seem to respond when I told him that I wanted to come home. He couldn't respond when I asked about my mother. And I thought how strange the phone call had seemed. I remember falling into a kind of depression over the next few days, and waited for the regatta to end and at least return to Sands Point, which I did.

A few days later I got the news. My father came to me privately for a talk and, honestly, though I'd had many "talks" with my stepfather, private talks with my father had never taken place. I knew this was going to be bad but I listened as best I could. He told me my mother had died. And, in fact, she had been buried. I just couldn't believe what he was telling me.

Good Lord! We need to grieve, to mourn, to cry real tears in order to live again. I never had that chance. I never got to say goodbye to my beloved mother. When my father told me, I went dead. I never felt a thing for the longest time, although there were feelings deep within me that would beckon for healing for years to come.

For the rest of my life in the Shorewood Drive house, we would never talk of my prior life. I realize that the day I'd called Tal, my mother had just died and though funeral arrangements had been made, he no longer had the power or the right to communicate with me. It was all in my father's hands. So that was that. The life I'd known was over. Roots were severed, friends lost, possessions given away, all gone. But the oddest thing of it all was that despite death, the bond remained. She was taken before she grew old at 39, and I'll always remember her that way. I've never forgotten our mother-daughter love affair and the words that made the eternal an actual reality to me: "I love you through infinity and back again."

I was indeed abandoned over and over again. I may even carry some survivor's guilt, but eventually I would feel again. And I would feel passionately because, I suppose, that's just who I am in spite of or even because of my life's challenges. I would cry again. I'd cry for my mother and I would be okay with those tears. We humans can transcend the most amazing hardships. And of course, we can and often do transform as a result... I came to live by the concept, "The wound is the way"! I suppose, however, my view of the world and developing character would have to be somewhat unique in the face of never having known normalcy. Certainly, while most kids my age were simply struggling with pecking orders and developing egos, I was living with very real dramas. It makes a person different to lead a different life. But one of the tragedies of my mother's death besides her death was that it may have destroyed the possibility of a healthy, loving relationship with my father. And I will regret that till my dying day.

I lived there for four more years and, though depression had taken hold in some way, I managed to live my life without much difficulty. How could life go on? It did. There was very little bonding between me and my new family. My sister was soon to graduate and go to college, and Helen and Clyde lived a somewhat self-involved life that had little to do with their children unfortunately.

I do remember, though, our family dinners. I rather enjoyed them, though I never talked, ever. I think what I liked most was that for whatever it was worth, these dinners were always entertaining. There was humor in the house, and as insane as it was, it was nonetheless lively. My father had the wildest sense of humor I'd ever seen the likes of, and sometimes a bit appalling. He had no sensors. And young Evan, who was truly a genius was as wickedly funny as any comedian I've yet to witness! Truly, our family dinners were always full of laughter. They were all witty in their own way.

I was glad for the humor but clearly my father didn't know how to reach out to me and was ill equipped to connect on a soulful level. I believe in many ways he was a child himself. All I knew was that I was growing up under the "tutelage" of parents who had not quite grown up themselves and created an atmosphere of chaos.

The epitome of the craziness on Shorewood Drive took the cake, with wild late-night parties that I will have to leave to your imagination. Those were "different" days, I suppose. But they thought nothing of their loud and raucous behavior that kept the rest of the household up at night. It would seem an impossible thing to get used to, but we did, and eventually we would just shake our heads and laugh. Most of the dramatic events of my life had taken place by now, but the life I witnessed on Shorewood Drive was as wild as anyone could imagine.

ANAM CARA

"All of us at some point had a vision of our existence
as something unique, untransferable, and very precious.
This revelation almost always takes place during adolescence.
Octavio Paz

The treasure of my teenage years came by way of friends that still remain in my heart. Perhaps, however, I found my salvation in what Joseph Campbell referred to as "one's bliss". And yes, I found my truest friend and meaning in the arts. When I think back through all these years, back to every phase, I realize the one thing I came into this world with that could not be severed was my calling to the arts, and not just one avenue, but all. In the beginning it was the music that I craved. I couldn't get enough of it. That first year I had entered the Sands Point school system, some friends and I would get together and when we were not making trouble, we'd make music. I have many memories walking down the long, gorgeous Sands Point roads in the early evening singing songs together. Near the end of that school year, they had announced the upcoming talent show. Naturally I put our names down and we started rehearsing. I knew a little guitar and actually taught myself to sing to Joan Baez and Joni Mitchell records. Such artists were mentors for a young soprano. I'd spend hours in my room listening to singers and singing along.

My father loved my voice, and though I made sure to keep my door shut, he'd always let me know that he'd heard me and was so proud. "You sing like a bird, like a bird," he'd say. I was happy for his opinion but I wish he'd have left it at that, because he'd make me sing for anyone and everyone who'd come to the house. The number of times he'd wake me from the dead of sleep at 2:00 in the morning to sing for company became maddening. I loved to sing, but I hated that.

In any event, my friends and I sang in the talent show and won a place; I really don't remember which. But apparently that night an audience member, affiliated with an off-Broadway show in the works, saw me and had been impressed enough to contact me. They were auditioning girls my age for a brand-new musical. I'd been to a few Broadway shows by now, and this seemed like the opportunity of a lifetime. I had grown up on all the great musical comedy artists of the time: Judy Garland, Fred Astaire, Gene Kelly, and Danny Kaye. The list goes on and on and I adored them all. Not only did they lift me out of the blues, but they inspired me to follow in their footsteps. I wanted to be them.

Truth be told, my first choice would have been to be a ballerina. It was my great desire to study when I lived with Mado and Papa Sam and performed for imaginary audiences in my little tutu. That desire stayed with me, but for some reason Tal and Mady wouldn't allow it. They'd even gone so far as to bribe a shoe salesman into stating that I didn't have dancer's feet, that I had extra bones in my feet and would never dance. I'll never forget it.

Well, now at 13, perhaps it was too late to dance, but oh, could I sing. And when I did, I felt the grace of the divine soar through me. Some say music is God. Well, I think all the arts are some form of channeled spirit. The performing arts is actually embodied spirit in a sense and for me, a way to find coalescence and grace. At 13 years old, I couldn't put it into words. But I felt it. And I understood the deep meaning it had in my life.

Anyway, I auditioned and I got the part. I sang and I danced and I acted in my first professional off-Broadway show at 13. This was my bliss and though I explored just about everything in the performing arts, singing was the beginning and it was salve for my tender soul.

High school came and I joined the varsity choir under the direction of Jerald Stone. In one's life, if you're a performer, many mentors appear and they leave their print, their gifts, their knowledge, or even their inspiration. Jerry was the first in my life, my musical director. He was the one that I would see first thing every single morning till the day I graduated high school and moved on. I remember without fail, each morning, still in bed, I'd clear my voice and start warming up. Every morning I'd arrive at school and begin my day communicating with the heavens through song. This was a very good choir and I was blessed to be a part of it. We sang in venues of all sorts, locally and in Manhattan, as Jerry had been in the profession before becoming a teacher, and obviously still had contacts.

One year he asked me to audition for the all-state choir, a very big to-do in Albany, New York. It would be an honor to be chosen, as only the very best singers and musicians were taken from New York State. I guess I was one of them because in fact, I was chosen. It was a spectacular experience. Over the years one thing led to the next and I wound up with the leads in the school musicals, like Eliza in My Fair Lady and the role of Monica in Gian Carlo Menotti's The Medium. We were producing very sophisticated shows ranging from musical comedy to opera. In fact, when the time came for choosing my higher education, I had quite a time deciding whether to go into opera or acting. In the end it was the latter that caught my attention, but often I wonder what it would have been like to dedicate my life to the opera. Singing kept me alive back then. And life was becoming rich because of it.

Often Jerry would bring friends in from New York City to lend a more professional eye during our rehearsals. I had been aware of his friend Wayne who I had met my first year of high school, but hadn't gotten to know at that time. I never assumed this funny, wild man would come to mean so much to me. But in fact, my relationship with Wayne became one of the most important in my life. I felt in a way that I had been discovered by him, and perhaps it was his early faith in me that engendered the confidence I needed to go into the profession. He had inspired many young performers and continues to do so these many years later, still living in New York City. And by no means a wealthy man, he continues to support young talent either by producing them or opening doors that they themselves might never have found a way to. He certainly opened doors for me. I came to know years and years later that not all theatre people are as pure at heart as Wayne. Though fascinating souls, theatre folk are, or so many seem to be ruled by their egos, I'm sorry to say. I never found this to be the case with Wayne. Whatever eccentricities this very theatrical man had, a competitive or jealous side to him was not present in his nature. Wayne took me under his wing and to this day I am grateful. I so appreciated his support, particularly at the time, because my own father didn't have any.

I'd like to take a moment to speak of this because ultimately, Clyde was not only non-present but terribly judgmental. And I felt at the effect of his judgement for many years. It seemed odd in a way coming from such a personality as he himself led the life of the free spirit. So, I never was quite able to comprehend that Clyde, the wildest of them all, had so often judged my friends. Maybe it was just a generation gap but to Clyde, their hair was either too long, their skin too dark, they were too dumb or they were too poor. There was a friend amongst them all who really got his goat, and actually when I think back to the story, I laugh out loud at the way it all played out.

One of my very best friends back then was a fellow artist by the name of Clayton Campbell, who incidentally was every bit as eccentric as I, and maybe as eccentric as my own father. I always thought he was a beautiful rebel though, with a most unique mind, and the perfect friend for me. In a way, we adopted each other. In any event, Clayton was experimenting with full-body casting at the time and needed a place to do his work. Well, I have to admit it was awfully naïve of me to think that I could offer our basement to him, but no one ever went down there. The pool table was no longer used, so I offered it up in the name of good will to an artist in need. For some time, friends were in and out of our house and somehow Clyde never knew that his old pool table was being used to make full-sized sculptures, that is until one day a failed life-sized sculpture of Jesus Christ on a cross wound up on our front yard.

My father was incensed, and I admit this had crossed the line, especially since it remained there for something like a month before it was hauled away. I'm tickled by this memory though, as outrageous as it was. My father couldn't stand Clayton but I wonder what he would have thought, that one day, Clayton who had his start with the making of Jesus on his basement pool table, would become a highly respected, world-renowned artist. Hah!

That image of Jesus fills me with laughter, as sacrilegious as it may have been. I should think that Jesus himself would have found some humor in it. I can't blame my father for his response, but the sad truth was that the whole nature of our relationship seemed to be grounded in nothing else but his negative assessment of my friends, but more importantly of me (at least that's how it felt).

I always wondered why he'd been such a sweet and loving father when I was little, and I know like me, he would have wanted more. It was sad for both of us, but perhaps this was the obvious outcome intensified by the fact that we had never gotten close when we should have, after my mother's death.

I thank God I had my friends, my talents, and after all was said and done, where my father lacked a sense of love and appreciation for me, Wayne made up for in spades. We are drawn to different people for many different reasons and often we don't see it till later. In many ways, Wayne had become my surrogate father. I know I needed him, and I think he needed in a way to take that very role with many young people.

When I think of others who helped me through those times, I have to say that not only was I blessed with a surrogate father, but perhaps a loving mother too. Now and then I would find comfort in my visits to Papa Sam and Mado. It was never easy to get to them, as they lived in New Jersey, but with them, George and their young Daniel, I found some remnant of my own life. More importantly, Mado and I developed a very rich relationship that grew till the day she died. She always called me the daughter that she never had, and she too gave to me something of the mother-daughter love and the nurturing that I so needed.

High school was drawing to a close and at 17, I was ready to move on. I know I was taken care of in those days, but aside from sharing our love of sailing, my father and I shared little but aggravation for each other. His drinking got worse and the charm he'd once had was being taken over now by more brutish traits. Unfortunately for him, he never wished to examine his own life, and because of pride, he lost out. Helen was the second wife to leave him and during my last year with him, he carried on an affair with another drinking partner named Fran. I could no longer stand the kind of craziness that went on in that household. He presumed to judge me harshly, but given the circumstances, I couldn't help but judge him. And it was very hard to allow myself the right to need him as any teenage daughter moving into the world naturally would. I always felt torn and I felt terrible shame in needing him.

That summer, however, whether it was out of guilt, obligation, or pure generosity, my father gave me an extraordinary graduation gift by way of one of the best vacations imaginable. I was blessed to have found a lifelong friend who meant the world to me then... and means the world to me even now... Karen, and I had been joined at the hip for some time. We practically lived at each other's houses... Her parents were Norwegian and had kept a home on the Island of Golta close to Bergen. I'd heard so much from her about Norway over the years. So, when she invited me to join her family for a month, I happily accepted, despite the fact that I'd have to forego my graduation ceremony... I hardly cared... The idea of going to the land of the midnight sun with my very best friend was too splendid for words... I still hold memories of that beautiful country. For someone who loved the sea, this was paradise. I'll never forget going out with the island seamen net fishing in the early evenings and traveling through fjords and mountains into Lapland. I still have a longing for travel, the likes of that. We had a magnificent month together and I could have seen myself living abroad somewhere very easily. After all, most of my family was European. At 17, nothing was going to keep me from the adventure and the independence that I'd so longed for. That trip remains one of the greatest gifts Clyde ever gave me, and I'm forever grateful.

INDEPENDENCE

It was 1969 and a vibrant time for young people, to say the least. It really felt to me that we were the heartbeat of the nation in so many ways. My generation existed in a special time capsule never to be seen again once the pendulum took its turn away from peace love and understanding. We had a kind of wild spirit and a sense of freedom that led some to political activism. The hippie movement advocated self-expression and the right to show up and stand up. It was a unique time in history for sure and I was more than happy to be a part of it.

The idea of "being an individual" still had huge merit. Perhaps some remnants of the beatnik era remained intact. I know they did for me... These times were the perfect environment for an eccentric soul like me, who needed to be honored for who she was. And I was such a nature child that flower power seemed to me in true alignment with the natural world. Perhaps I escaped the madness of my household, by leaning into another kind of madness that only my generation knew. But we had love on our side, and a strong desire to come together in celebration. We escaped judgment and prejudice and we lived openly at least for a while.

After Norway, I headed up to a little town near Woodstock called West Shokan. I stayed for one month with a commune and did everything in my power to break free of whatever troubles still had a hold on me. I threw myself into the tribal experience it offered and loved that aspect of it. And upstate New York was magnificent. What a way to initiate my independence, with fellow free spirits living in the wilds.

That summer I got to go abroad, live like a hippie, experience LSD, MDA, go to the Woodstock concert, and lose my virginity all at once. God, talk about freedom! This life lasted only a couple of months, but that's all I needed. I will always carry an image of my summer of emancipation living in my green maxi dress, barefoot, with long auburn hair dangling past my shoulders. And for the daughter of a man who had placed one's meaning in the acquisition of money; my short stint panhandling was the perfect symbol of defiance. A kid has to break away, each in his own way. And maybe it's all just ritual, but it would seem to be a necessary initiation to one's transition into young adulthood. I had my initiation in Woodstock while living the life of a hippie… and at the same time, I managed to transcend my world of judgment that liked to squeeze the life out of me.

Now I was ready to move on to New York City and begin my adult life. And I would do so with a new-found self-esteem and excitement for the adventure that I was about to enter into. I was coming into my own, and my own was ever so much better than what came before. It had to be. It had to be better than alcoholism. It had to be better than divorce after divorce. It certainly had to be better than mental illness. But most especially, I needed it to be better than the devastating kind of illness that takes the life of beautiful mothers like mine before their time. Yes, I was coming into my own finally, and once and for all, I would have a sense of control over my destiny.

I moved to Manhattan near the end of that summer with Karen. My sister had a one bedroom on 26th and Lexington Ave. and she was moving in with her fiancé, Barry. Luckily, we already had a lease on the apartment. I loved this place. Cockroach infested as it was, it was mine for $206 a month, my first apartment! I could decorate it as I wished; I could come and go as I wished; and I could invite the sort of friends that I wished. I was free to be me at last!

The first thing I did was get a cat. This seemed to me terribly important. And though I went on many road-shows after schooling, I managed to keep Piewacket, otherwise known as "black thing," till she died at 16. Karen kept a pet too, a most unusual one, a woolly monkey who mostly lived in a big cage. But when he wanted to make a ruckus, as monkeys want, he'd get up on his little swing and pee across the room to the other wall. One never quite knew how to prepare or find a way to dodge the spray. Hah… we were crazy girls each in our own way loving our young lives in New York.

Karen was a year older and had been going to the School of Visual Arts already. I was now just entering The American Academy of Dramatic Arts, the school that I finally decided upon when my original plan to go to Carnegie Mellon fell through. Clyde had encouraged me to go this route instead of a traditional university. I'd always wanted to minor in psych and regret that I hadn't, but Clyde figured I'd get my training and then simply become a star. Success came easily to him; I'm sure he never assumed it wouldn't to me. In any event, he did encourage my acting career.

Oddly, however, my stepfather did not. Here's a pivotal story… I had rarely seen Tal over the years, but I did meet with him once after high school. I'd had a whole unresolved life that I'd never even said good-bye to, and he was part of that life. And I know he was devastated when my mother died and I was taken from him. It was time for us to finally get together and so we did. I don't know what I thought would come of it. He'd taken the father role for enough years that something inside of me wanted to share my plans of becoming an actress. But was I looking for approval? If so, I should have known I wasn't necessarily going to get it from him. Of course, my father wasn't the most emotionally supportive, but he did recognize that I had talent and had a right to explore my path. But when I told Tal about my plans, he lectured me. He lectured me as he always had. He couldn't help himself. I'd forgotten him through the years, but it all came back now, now that I was coming into my own. Naïvely I had invited him back into my life to dismiss me and to disapprove. It was extraordinary! But worse, after his long lecture, he had the audacity to say that my mother wouldn't have approved either. That was the clincher. That cruel statement struck a nerve within me so deeply that my mind and body simply flipped!

While stuck in New York City traffic I had a meltdown the likes of which I'd never had before. I became hysterical. And I summoned a power from within that I'd never known existed inside me. It was as if I'd come upon a particular combination of feelings that were absolutely combustible, and I just went off the deep end. I exploded with rage then opened the car door and fled through the streets. I remember running like the wind with tears flooding down my face. My mother wouldn't approve. My beloved mother would not approve of my life! The thought was too much to bear!

In the end, here's what occurs to me when I think back to that moment in time. I realize something vitally important had been given birth to that day; my power. Oh, it would take a lifetime to learn just how to hold on to it and more importantly how to use it. But at the time this experience was perhaps part of my new-found freedom. Perhaps along with power, the full extent of one's life force comes into being and that fiery passion needs its voice in the world.

In any event my warrior spirit came to light that day and brought with her a strength that hadn't been there before. I was staking a claim for my life, and it almost felt like I had to set the wilds of my nature free again, after terrible childhood tamings to come into my own and feel truly alive.

As it happens, passion and power served me in other ways that I wouldn't have expected. But the best of what I'd have to offer as an actress came from this well of emotion, along with my deep, emerging soul. Acting would become an amazing container for all that I had learned and all that I felt about life itself.

Manhattan in the early days was like being in a faraway country considering where I'd been that summer of '69. Traveling to Lapland via Norway and playing the hippie in Woodstock are memories I'll cherish always, but I was living on my own in New York City and I was about to step onto the path of my biggest dream of all, a career in the performing arts. I threw away my hippie garb, moved on to my mini mod skirts, and began my two years at The American Academy of Dramatic Arts.

Those days were more fun than I can say. The Academy offered a ready-made community of friends and like minds so vital for a young person moving out into the world. And two years of a marvelous program that ranged from scene study, theatre history, makeup and tech and improv; the list goes on. And if you were asked back to the second year, that second year took the form of a repertory company with ongoing productions to which New York City agents would attend. I loved it!

I remember that what originally attracted me to this school over the others was actually their program cover. It seemed ever so much more artful, and it appealed to me for reasons that I can't say I understood back then, but I had already been making most of my choices out of instinct. As I said before, I might have made a career of singing, but it was the artwork on the program of the American Academy that clinched the deal. It was a photo of three figures posed together in a most intriguing composition. They were all in masks and black unitards. It reminded me of something, I couldn't quite pinpoint what, but the impression was strong. What that photo had to do with acting, I couldn't imagine; what it had to do with the Academy I couldn't fathom. Yet, in a way, it kind of called to me and so I followed in good faith.

Memories of my first days there remain present. I remember the lobby where so many new faces of good-looking young actors met and moved through to their various classes. I remember getting my bearings there, the first day while observing my fellow acting students, some of which might wind up being good friends. It struck me how some looked as disoriented as I and others, the seniors, seemed to own the school. It was almost intimidating. They were only a year older, but they'd had their initial year, and so they naturally assumed they were stars. Perhaps some of them would become stars; in fact, some did. But certainly, at this time, that illusion of fame merely represented budding egos to which we juniors believed to be true. We would have our day in the hall of fame once we were seniors too. And I'm certain these 30-some odd years later, the case is the same. We looked up to those seniors and when some of them were handed contracts from Universal Studios or became overnight stars like Kate Jackson who went on to do Charlie's Angels, we figured the sky was the limit, and maybe we would get there too. Many others went straight to the top. The one in particular that I personally rooted for was Bobby Davis. He was a small, sweet boy with an amazing talent. Talk about a deep and passionate well of raw emotion. I was blown away by his work and knew he'd be a force in town, and indeed he was. He was the young, up and coming actor who had the kind of success that inspired us all and gave us the confidence that anything was possible... Unfortunately, Bobby (Brad Davis) died all to soon of AIDS, having succumbed to the dark shadow side of Hollywood in those days.

AIDS claimed the lives of so many back then, and it viciously took his. I'm sure most of us who began our careers back then suffered the loss of oh so many friends. It came with the territory of being a performer, whether you were an actor, a singer, or a dancer... a devastating marker of our times. I lost many friends but had formed some rather deep bonds that still enrich my life to this day.

The truest bond I'd formed was with my dear friend, Jane. I was sitting in one of the school theatres for a scene study class when a beautiful girl came late to class on crutches due to a recent foot surgery.

We, the class, had been performing our audition monologues for each other, and I have to say, Jane's entrance on crutches seemed far more compelling than what I'd witnessed on the stage. I remember her well and I guess she remembered me too from the start. Even girlfriends can find an attraction to each other, and sometimes it comes from an unknown place. You never know. But if it's a soul connection, the relationship can last a lifetime and find its purpose beyond the initial companionship, though Jane and I did become great companions.

I remember her short black hair and form that was quite the opposite of mine. We became instant friends and Jane moved into my 26th Street apartment when Karen moved out. And our lifetime friendship began. Jane and I got to know each other well and compared notes on our childhood traumas of which there were many. We had great times and some scuffles too – you don't get to be a soul sister without scuffles, especially when soul sisters are equally deep and intense. She was to remain my special friend forever, through thick and thin, and through long distance. We have watched each other's remarkable growth and perhaps even lent a hand in each other's growth by way of love, nurturing and inspiration. Jane and I always honored each other's spiritual journey as well as creative. And Jane seemed to understand my surprisingly mystical stories when others might have considered them eccentric... like the time I stood before the bathroom mirror and swore I literally encountered my soul! Jane got it! She was a true gift that came out of my years at the Academy.

As juniors, many of us shared classes, and certainly bonded through the experience of being independent for the first time. We did a little studying, and a whole lot of partying. I recall many of those school friends well, though I never saw them again after the Academy. We were close then... at least we thought we were.

Kids that age are wild, let's face it. I always wonder how they make it through young adulthood when caution is thrown to the ethers. And of course, in the name of freedom, they go to hell with themselves. Freedom! I'm not certain I even knew what it truly meant. I just knew I craved it and so I simply followed the wind.

Anyway, the Academy really was great. I loved everything about it and although romance never developed past a good deal of fooling around, I was perfectly happy with the way things were. I wasn't ready for a real relationship even though I believed I was. Just as well. I threw myself into the acting world, and even claimed that I would never marry and that the only husband I'd ever take would be theatre.

The Academy offered a well-rounded education in the theatre without the distractions of a liberal arts school. It was fairly intensive as a result, I suppose. But when I look back objectively, I must admit that the best training I received there or anywhere else I might add was not from a traditional acting class at all; it was from an extraordinary man named Paul J. Curtis who was the founder and director of an art form called American Mime. And the photo that I had been so drawn by on the cover of the school brochure was his. In fact, that photo was from one of his plays named "The Lovers", and actually I would one day play the role of the female. Little did I know at the time that I would become a significant member of his company, and that he would become my lifetime mentor.

His classes fascinated me. They were tough, really tough. But I think I've always liked toughness in all I've taken on in life, because of the serious and authentic nature of the kind of lessons one can learn as a result... There was much to learn from Paul. He had described a curriculum unlike any other, yet had combined the principles of some of the greatest disciplines ever: Stanislavsky, Grotowski, Chekhov, Decroux, maybe even Martha Graham; a little Marceau, though pantomime was hardly utilized. No, this was an art form that fused organic acting and movement skills in a way never seen before, and to master it, one would have to devote oneself to it. I remember he always used to say: "The days of mastering anything at all are gone, gone!" Even the shoe cobbler has thrown his skills away with the advent of manufacturing. Everyone prefers the easy route, but American Mime required mastery and a will to learn, to grow, and actually become a master craftsman. All of this appealed to my pure and serious nature. The challenge seemed enormous, yet worthwhile too because the art form was utterly mesmerizing. The Academy implemented the American Mime curriculum because they knew this was the one course that literally dealt with one's instrument and internal landscape. Perhaps that was why it was so tough. The great rewards of exploring one's internal equipment takes courage, because you can't succeed without being willing to become vulnerable, deeply vulnerable. And you needed to surrender your ego in the process. This was above all the most intriguing aspect of Paul J. Curtis' course. Because of that I was terrified of him yet utterly drawn to him as well. Maybe it appealed to that deep well of passion that I had come to know. Maybe I knew that this was a way to not only tap it, but to use it creatively somehow. To enter into such a game, however, would take a certain degree of freedom. Freedom again. Yes, in fact, the subject of freedom may very well have been the center of the art form. It certainly became clear that without attaining freedom as an actual acting skill, you couldn't possibly go terribly far with the performing art. American Mime was a complete and complex methodology that would take years to fully understand and get good at. And during our first year at the Academy, we merely scratched the surface. Our work in the area of freedom was one of the most fascinating, and it got me thinking what a vast and mysterious subject it was. It was the theme of my mother's life and indeed, mine. But my early work with Paul Curtis opened the door to understanding its nuances and what it would mean to me as an actress, an artist and as a human being.

I think I was becoming more and more conscious in those days, but was still just blowing in the wind so to speak. Life itself made impressions on me and I would follow the call. American Mime made such an impression. There was no doubt it called my name and had much to do with the journey of my soul. I had much to learn. And Paul Curtis was the one to teach me. I got a taste while receiving some curious lectures about the human condition and engaging in equally curious exercises of all sorts. If we worked hard, whether we knew what we were doing or not, we'd be lucky to walk away a bit more in touch with our instruments and ourselves. I never forgot Paul. He talked about life in ways that always struck a chord of truth within me, and I didn't even know why. Perhaps he was appealing to my own artist's soul that was only just developing consciousness.

But if these were the most valuable teachings of my two years at the Academy, the second year in repertory was the most fun. I wish I'd been more conscious of keeping photographs. I seem to have nothing but snapshots in my head of the various roles I played. One stands out. It was the role of Laurette in Another Part of the Forest by Lillian Hellman. That was when I realized that despite my New York upbringing and long, ethnic nose, I had a knack for the southern ladies with a natural inclination for such characters. Had I looked the part I might have had an easier time of it professionally, but somehow my looks never quite matched the sort of roles that I was right for. It meant nothing back then, but would be the bane of my existence later. No, I'd never be the traditional ingénue, middle American housewife, or any number of leading ladies with an ethnic face like mine. But I could play them. Oh, could I play them! Tennessee Williams must have had my soul in mind when he wrote about all those fascinating women with their eccentricities... too bad.

That year I also did Roar of the Greasepaint, Smell of the Crowd and a few others. The role that got attention and caught my attention, however, was Thea in Hedda Gabbler. I got my first real taste of what it meant to "live the character". The evening of our first performance was uncanny. When I learned that my beloved Eljert was dead, tears exploded from my lower depths. We'd been rehearsing this play, but that hadn't happened before, not like this. But in front of the audience as if in a shared ritual, I fully opened up to the depths of Ibsen's character by fully opening up to the depths of my being. Maybe this had been possible because of my unfortunate connection with death; or maybe it was a well of tears that I'd never cried when my father told me that my mother died. I couldn't understand, but what I did know was that my experience on that stage was in a peculiar way, liberating. It was somehow bigger than life, though my own life was bigger than most drama. This, however, felt more meaningful than the mundane existence of day-to-day living, even at its best.

It doesn't always happen this way, but when an actor is at his best and "in the moment" he is in what is known as a "creative state", a state of spontaneity and focus, a state of connectedness. The true art of acting begins here. This is it in a nutshell. We're after a kind of coalescence and perhaps a certain transcendence at least from the ego... This is freedom! Yes, this is freedom.

My friend Wayne had come to that night's performance and I remember how he held me after the show. I couldn't stop crying and didn't know why. But it felt like years of pent-up feelings had broken loose and I had no choice but to let it out. They say to play the instrument well, the actor begins and ends with vulnerability. It is our aim to make ourselves raw and though I don't feel there's any merit in indulgence, any good actor will tell you there's a therapeutic component to the actors' process. I always felt blessed to have found my way to the arts because they really did save my life.

During that time, I kept up my friendship with Wayne. Like a guide looking in on me from time to time, he always had a nurturing eye. He also took me into the heartbeat of New York City culturally speaking in a way that I may never have known without him. We went to the theatre when money was there, as well as some of the best eateries. The only way to eat as well would either mean moving to Europe, or learning to cook gourmet. I certainly was inspired to learn the art of gourmet and become a head chef in my own home. What can I say? Wayne and I had gourmet tastes and shared in common a sophisticated taste in many things, from good food to good theatre and art, and interior design.

Wayne seemed to be expert at so many things. Perhaps he was the first Renaissance man I'd ever encountered. I'd never considered that in myself, though I certainly had a good eye, good taste, and an insatiable thirst for good culture. Wayne was more than happy to introduce me to it. I'll never forget the first show he took me to when I was still a kid in high school actually. I took the train into Manhattan and met him down at a little theatre called the Village Gate. This evening in the West Village, I got a taste for what life could be like if I chose to live here. It felt alive. And speaking of which, the very play that he took me to see that night was "Jacques Brel is Alive and Well and Living in Paris". What an experience! I had never seen anything quite like it. Wayne had been to see it numerous times and it was easy to understand why. The impact it made on me was powerful. I had no idea at the time that Wayne would one day produce it himself and I would sing in his first rendition, coming full circle to do it again many years later several times. In any event, I first saw it in '68 when I was just a girl.

Early experiences like these can make a lasting impression and influence your life and your thinking. Jacques Brel did. The funny thing is, I was told a couple of years later by somebody that I actually looked like one of Brel's daughters. A Belgian friend of his had done some directing at the Academy and told me that my resemblance to the daughter was uncanny. It always made me feel a little closer to

Brel. Who knows what bonds us to strangers? I only know that when we resonate on deep levels with anyone in this world, be it socially or with a mentor, a celebrity, a fellow artist, or even an author, the connection feels almost spiritual. There have been many I have felt that way about. Jacques Brel was one.

Anyway, my two years at the Academy were coming to a close. Graduation came and went with a pomp and circumstance much highlighted by the presence of one of my favorite actors on the planet, Danny Kaye. I felt ushered into the professional world by his merely being there.

Some people got contracts; some got agents; some became famous; I did not. Perhaps I never would be commercial enough, but I worked. I had a piece of the New York pie, and it was good. I suppose initially I thought I'd be a star like a few others. I suspect all actors imagine themselves on the Johnny Carson Show, and if it doesn't happen, you either quit or you find other ways to develop a creative way of life. And a creative life was absolutely what meant the most to me. And as long as I was in New York, I was a vital part of that culture.

Auditioning became a part of it all, as was working on the craft continuously. In the beginning I was nearly always on the road with this, that or the other. Of course, my father had never considered such travel to be part of the actor's life, but it is. It made him crazy each time I'd move out of an apartment and into the next. I was beginning to look like a gypsy or a vagabond, but that is a very typical life for many actors, singers and dancers. Some of them live their whole career on the road. After a while it ceased to have any appeal to me. I think I'd been so uprooted as a child, that some groundedness at home would become necessary. Until then, I would tour for a few more years, all over the States, mostly with musicals. I did two different tours with Fiddler on the Roof, a no-brainer to cast someone like me in the role of Tzeitel. The second tour was fun, actually, with Jerry Jarod, the last Tevia in the long-running Broadway production. There were other tours but, of course, the one that meant the most was Jacques Brel. It was quite an extraordinary gift to be involved; an honor actually for someone as young as I. Unfortunately, however, when I look back objectively, I believe I was way too young. I was certainly too undisciplined or prepared for the hard work that this would take. I suppose I sang alright, but was never able to take full ownership of the role. This was my first experience in the theatre that felt beyond me. And worse, my "failure," (and it did feel like a failure) was with this most beloved piece, Jacques Brel. Wayne who had produced and directed, seemed to have lost all faith in me after so many years believing in me. What a blow! It seemed our good times together would fall away forever more... I'd had the best of times with Wayne from all-night dinners with interesting theatre folk to readings of Gertrude Stein's "The Making of the Americans". I had even lived with him periodically along with other young protégés like Keith Berger and Billy Forsyth. I remember those times so fondly. This was the end of an era with Wayne, and we barely talked for years after. That was hard for me, really hard.

But of course, it had its purpose and its lesson. Life is tough sometimes and whether non-theatre folks understand it or not, life in the theatre is not all play. Some of it is; a lot of it is not. We have to develop our psyches well, get thick skins yet remain sensitive. The issue of the actor/artist's ego is an interesting one. The life we have to conquer puts us more on the edge than anyone can imagine. Our courage and our confidence are always being challenged through rejections, or less-than-wonderful reviews. Eventually I would come to understand that the good reviews could have their own ill effect as well.

Many of us go into the arts for reasons we don't quite understand in the beginning. Initially, some of us are called to it, like me. I think it's the soul that answers that call. It fulfills a deeper need and an appetite to express something of the human spirit and human condition. Hopefully we illuminate something of that to our audience. The downside to it all, in my opinion, is that the ego has to get involved. Certainly, it has to, in order to go for the limelight, come hell or high water... and it has to in order to stay there. Even when the feedback is glowing, the sad thing is it can take you off the pure path that you were meant to be on in the first place. Then the challenge will be to find your authentic way again. In any event along the way, we actors have to fight against all that stuff that deflates us and all the stuff that inflates us, to remain true artists. Indeed, living in accord with the Great Creator takes some growing up. Sometimes we need those lessons that hurt; sometimes they push us deeper. As much as my Brel experience hurt, I tend to think that it helped me grow beyond a certain immaturity.

In any event, I returned to NY, and went on with my life. This is how it goes sometimes, doesn't it? We believe we have solid footing on our path when the unexpected occurs, and we're nudged in another direction altogether. I must say, although a turn of events brought me to a brand new set of circumstances, when I look back I realize that what followed instead of a year or two on the road with Brel was a vitally important time in my life... Ah, how fate and destiny play their hand!

I remember at the time I had a most intriguing dream. I'll never forget it. I dreamt I'd found a new spiritual practice that was meant to bring one into enlightenment. You literally had to turn yourself inside-out, and I don't mean like the moves of a Yogi or a contortionist. This was literal. But of course, the dream was symbolic and came at another transformational moment in my life. This dream stands out in my mind because it strikes a chord of truth for the journey that I'd been on, and what it would turn into down the road. These days were filled with spiritual adventures.

Though I no longer lived on 26th Street, I kept up a friendship with a young man I'd met there. He himself was an actor who had lived and worked in the building as a superintendent. After a couple of years of flirtation, we finally got together. He and I had a fairly loose affair for years, but definitely one that had purpose beyond being lovers. Gordon introduced me to Buddhism.

Back then New York was all about actors shakabukuing each other and learning about this Buddhist form called Nissuran Shoshu. Chanting before an altar was an opening to spiritual practice for me, but perhaps the best thing about it at the time was meeting some really great people.

I chanted, I think, for about one year, but didn't stick with it. At the time I lived in the West Village on Hudson and 11th. I loved that street right next to The White Horse Tavern! I never thought of that street as seedy or dangerous but my chanting days ended there when I came home one night to find my apartment had been broken into. The door had literally been taken off its hinges and thrown flat on my living room floor. Black footprints were everywhere, and whatever was left behind was in an utterly ravaged state. My cat was howling on my fire escape. The only thing left intact, interestingly enough, was my Buddhist temple. But nonetheless, I didn't feel I could stay there. I left that night and went to Mado and Papa Sam for refuge.

I returned to New York eventually and though I'm a little fuzzy about the time line and the various apartments I lived in, I wound up again in the Gramercy area, this time on 24th Street. I no longer chanted, but a palpable desire to ground a spiritual practice of exploration and ritual became as natural as anyone could imagine. And I suppose as a result, I was starting to have the most psychically powerful dreams, psychic experiences, and almost constant synchronicity. Interestingly enough, though I wasn't much of a reader in those days, I came across a book that seemed to find its way to me. Talk about synchronicity. This book was about the man who fashioned, or better said, realized the concept. I was already fascinated by psychology, certainly my own, and naturally that of the many characters I had dissected by now as an actor. But I didn't know of this particular author till this book. So, why would I have picked his autobiography? I suppose for the very same reason I went to the Academy – I was once again drawn to something about, of all things, the cover. In this case however, it was the simple face of the author that captured my attention; Carl Jung!

In any event, I dug in. I don't think that I put that book down except for a few nights of necessary sleep. Carl Jung spoke to me. So much of what he had to say I think I had been longing to hear expressed. I felt I knew this man. I must have had a lifetime with him. His theories all alluded to in this book struck such a chord with me, that I felt somehow validated... validated for my experience of life and for my view of it. I had to know more.

Through much reading and eventual therapy, I did become a devotee of his work, and it led to the exploration of very much more. The Jungian way, if there is one, I suppose, made all the sense in the world for someone like me, an artist, a spiritual seeker, and plainly a girl who still needed to work out her crazy childhood. All I know is that after reading "Dreams, Memories, and Reflections", I was hooked forever more to spiritual psychology. In fact, to this day, if you were to visit me, you would find my bookshelves spilling over with everything imaginable on the Human condition and all that would imply!

Perhaps the authors we're profoundly drawn to can be thought of as part of our soul's constellation. The ones that struck me even from the beginning, I suppose, appealed to my inner mystic. They all remain my heroes for sure. As a girl Hermann Hess enraptured me like no other and informed me of a most spiritual being within my soul that would take precedence through my entire life. And then there was Isadora Duncan who to this day became an idol to the resonating Goddess of love and freedom within.

And certainly, while studying acting, which for all intents and purposes is the study of the human psyche and soul, I began reading everything I could get my hands on in the field of psychology and such. Yes, I read everyone from Joseph Campbell to James Hillman, Rollo May, Ernest Becker, Viktor Frankl, Rumi, Rilke, and on and on and on!

I've been taken or perhaps led by so many mentors, extraordinary poets, artists, and philosophers in my life. And, to my mind, they reflected my soul in the process of becoming and developing over the years. I was drawn to anyone who devoted himself to the journey of man which I suppose I could call… my devotion as well.

I'd been in New York for enough time now to call it home. I continued to audition, but already knew my chances were slim at that time, and I wanted no more of the gypsy life. I didn't think much of the small rep companies, maybe out of naïveté, maybe out of snobbery. But I knew what was in my blood and I had to get back to it. I did a couple of off-Broadway shows and some showcases of new works, but nothing was all that terribly satisfying, nor did it pay well enough to keep pursuing. And then one day I thought of that old teacher of mine that had terrified yet fascinated me so at my first year at the Academy, Paul J. Curtis of The American Mime Theatre. I remember noting that his company was to perform at Town Hall, and so I went to see them. I was simply blown away. That work was awe-inspiring and it looked as impossible to perform as Olympic gymnastics. That was it. I had time on my hands while waiting around for the right Broadway role to come my way, so I was going to learn this magnificent art form. I stayed there for over ten full years, stepping in as the leading lady for awhile and teaching their course at many universities such as NYU, Yale and Cornell.

I grew up there under the tutelage of Paul Curtis and learned more from him about acting, movement, playwriting and life itself than anyone else with the possible exception of Carl Jung. It took me years to master and the program was more challenging than I can express. Paul was a force to be reckoned with, and while most students were intimidated by his acid assessment of their skill level, it rarely shook me. Perhaps that was because I believed in what he was teaching, or because ultimately, I knew my own potential, and I trusted the process. I can't say that's always the case these days, and I don't really know if it's a case of distrust in direction or that I don't quite have the chutzpah that I used to. What I know is that Paul was honest and never minced words. He demanded the very best from his students and practitioners, and knowing this was all I needed.

There was another wonderful book I'd stumbled upon right around that time. It seemed a perfect companion to my early mime training. It was called "The Courage to Create" by Rollo May. In it he explored the creative process in all its necessary stages. I often refer to this book and how it applies to the process of life itself. The title had really intrigued me and somehow, I came face-to-face once again with my life-long themes around the subject of freedom. Freedom and courage were cousins conceptually, but I knew there was something here that I needed to examine. In my training at The American Mime Theatre, I came to learn that of the many skills I'd have to acquire, the first and foremost was freedom, which I touched upon earlier. This was what I had just gotten a taste of when I was at the Academy that first year with Paul, but it certainly went further now. And I'd like to speak more about what I came to learn.

Without freedom, one could barely engage in the process. But it wasn't just one's ability to act boldly, or with verve that Curtis was addressing. I mean, I had verve and had no trouble taking risks. That was never the issue. What most people don't realize, unless they've engaged in a discipline like this, is that under social circumstances we function much of the time through the guise of confidence. We wear a mask that we're quite unconscious of. With shields and armor, we proudly hold our badge of courage, and claim to be free spirits, but are we? Most have little reason to look beneath the persona's mask. But artists, especially actors, do. This kind of exploration is not for sissies especially because you have to rattle the ego... maybe even slay it in order to reach what is known as one's essence. To me, this is where creativity and spirituality meet up.

86

A good actor comes to steer his vulnerability with an absolute confidence in a sense. This is an impossible way to function socially of course. I came to understand eventually that in the theatre there are all sorts of levels of abstraction, or styles I suppose. But social ought not to be one of them. At least this was what I was taught. With freedom one was able to move more deeply into one's essence or authentic self. And with that came connectedness and a degree of engagement with your fellow actor, your audience, the material, and yourself. In American Mime, performing from this place of essence was the caveat. There simply was no other way.

Paul was my true mentor in the ways of performance and the ways of my humanity. And he directly addressed my most vitally important spiritual themes such as Freedom… One of the things that came into question for me was the generation of which I was a part. It began to occur to me that the hippies of the times may only have scratched the surface of what it truly meant to be a free spirit! Though some ran streaking nakedly through streets, it didn't necessarily mean they had freedom. Most people aren't free enough to look each other squarely in the eye with an open and vulnerable heart, and connect. I would learn how and would frankly yearn for such connection in the "real world" forever more.

In any event, I worked hard at The American Mime Theatre, digging into every skill that I could attain till I was good enough to teach it and good enough to perform it.

The company became my family, my brothers and my sisters. I found I had the right temperament to be a member of a rep, and there was no competition as I would run into later down the road. Paul Curtis allowed no room for that sort of nonsense, perhaps because the social experience was not permitted into the studio. His notion was if we were to function in any way, shape or form, whether it be in rehearsal or company classes, the only way to work viably was from a creative state, and that state precluded the social way of functioning. In fact, a very well-defined warm-up proceeded every single session without fail, and it really is remarkable to me now, that since those days whenever I've done shows where the director attempted to take the company through a warm-up, it was inevitably poo-pooed and regarded as foolish. I know actors who have been insulted by it, but in reality, so much more can come of a creative session together when the social state is replaced by an actual creative state. So many, many skills were taught at The American Mime Theatre. And though I studied with several acting teachers I learned ever so much more about the performing arts during my 10 years with Paul.

One of the gems I walked away with was something rarely taught in this country: character acting and interplay... This work became invaluable for me on many levels. Not only did it allow me to explore my instrument and learn to craft wildly different roles, it struck a chord of fascination with me. I think it was because character work was absolutely grounded in the notion that we are oh so much more than our persona. In fact, "we are all made of the same stuff", and every sociological type resides within us. Of course, we were trained and trained others to access those "types" or "inner characters". But this work actually became the basis for so much more of my work in the healing arts, in my writing, and certainly in my world view. I could write an entire book about what this man had to offer. But I will say this; Paul was the very first to introduce me to the mere notion of many selves.

The truth is once I left the company, I walked away with invaluable knowledge that most people never understood. We all meet each other to share the present moment. We may bring our history to it, but most people see only what they can and vis-à-vis, their own world view. American Mime was a rare experience for all who studied and became practitioners.

Paul Curtis used to say, "It is our essence that counts. It is our soul that must find its expression each step of the way." One day I would leave The American Mime Theatre, but all the arts I was lucky enough to engage in indeed became the container of my soul. And it started with Paul...

Maybe I had to write an autobiography to give my time with the mime theatre proper due, less it slip away like all our lives as we move into the future. But I just have to say, it was Paul Curtis who taught me that most valuable life of all is the one that is somehow regarded creatively. Perhaps this was not his initial intention, but it was what I walked away with. Paul meant the world to me. I find myself quoting him almost daily, in fact, because his genius was remarkable... And because I'm more than proud to say he was my mentor.

I recall hearing a beautiful African fable once at a retreat some years ago. It was a myth used as an entry point for participants to speak of their own journey and how both intersected. This particular story told the tale of a child who'd gotten lost and separated from his family... Everyone who stood up and spoke to how they related, found different points within the myth that struck them, and their different experiences. I actually was surprised by where my mind went with the story... I learned something interesting about myself that day... Most spoke of their abandonment issues... (something we all know of to one degree or another) but they all related to the African tale that concluded with the tribe the child had found a way to bond with along the way. What I found myself saying was a little different than most... My separation from my family fueled my hunger for radical connections through my life, yes... absolutely. But as I "entered the story" I sought the feeling of family and tribe through the various mentors I found over the years... mentors of all sorts. They became precious members of my family... the ones related not necessarily by blood, but by resonance... Paul J Curtis was my first and perhaps my truest Mentor.

Those years were intertwined with a vibrant New York life. I was rarely bored. I continued classes to keep up my singing, though I hadn't sung professionally in some time. I did audition once in a while, and I suppose I'd have made it to Broadway had I put my focus there. Certainly, I had feedback that indicated it was just a matter of time. Hal Prince for instance had brought me in several times for a few of his plays. I almost landed the role of the old lady in Candide. In the end he told me that I was just too young, but that I would do well in my 40's because I was too young for my type. It always came down to my look. Though my other memory of near-Broadway success was when Tommy Tune wanted to cast me in one of his plays, but I'd really never studied dance, and so I couldn't decipher his choreography. He told me he tried to give me every chance, keeping me for hours when obviously I was not a trained dancer.

But it meant the world to me that I received praise from Tommy Tune! What does such a compliment mean when you still don't get the job? I smile when I remember that audition, and his recognition of me.

And then the one time I was offered a Broadway role, my answering service didn't get the message to me until two weeks later. I'll never forget when I spoke with the casting director. She was livid with me for not checking in myself on a daily basis. I had become very lax about my professional career. It didn't hold the same value as the Mime Theatre. But the truth is I didn't have the kind of drive necessary to make it, particularly knowing that my looks stood in the way of getting anything more than a chorus role. I never developed the balls for the business. They say a lot of artist types are like this. They're too sensitive for the business; they're circular by nature, right-brained I suppose. Those who do well are either lucky for their commercial appeal, or have fought like heck through thick and thin with thick skin to boot. I recall a teacher at the Academy telling us that we should be prepared to wait at least ten years before a break, and that would occur only after a lot of knocking down doors and networking. Well, it wasn't for me, and because of that, my path went in a very different direction than many of my actor friends. I regret some things but I got over my initial dreams of stardom, and threw myself into the deeper purpose of my life. What that would look like exactly, I didn't exactly know.

I always felt that one's happiness depended upon just a few ingredients really, but if even one was missing, life would feel somehow incomplete. First and foremost, you needed to have your health, then of course a roof over your head, and in order to pay for that roof, you had to have a job. Equally as important, and one may express this in slightly different terms, we all need a reason to get up in the morning and face the world. I believe that reason is found in one's bliss, as Joseph Campbell called it. It's the compelling drive within us that calls our name perhaps many times over through our lifetime. Many have to search for it. I never did, thank God. I just had to keep up with it as it led me to a whole variety of places. The last on the list is companionship, but more importantly, a primary relationship that at its best brings love into your life.

I couldn't complain. Maybe I wasn't rich like my father; maybe I'd never be. That was alright, at least for now. I had a roof over my head and always knew how to make my apartments cozy, and a single woman doesn't need a mansion anyway. I was lucky to be an artist. I was born with my bliss, and never in want of a muse. And health was not an issue, particularly because through the Mime Theatre, I kept in shape. And I have to say that the daily rituals that I engaged in kept me alive and stimulated, both mentally and spiritually. But indeed, my life was incomplete, and it was beginning to gnaw at me.

I had friendships and I have to give thanks to my treasured relationship with my friend Charna. We took care of each other for years, and not a day went by without long conversations on the phone or long visits together. I had even lived with her for a short while. And through the years, I kept up my friendship with Jane. I'd periodically go out to Connecticut to visit with her and her little girl, Jessica. These relationships were meaningful, especially because they ran deep. But I have to admit, though my life was rich and full on so many levels, I was indeed beginning to feel a certain emptiness inside that couldn't be filled by my lady friends. I had never had a successful relationship with a man, and the growing anxiety over it may have been the sign that I was finally ready for a little bit of love.

FIRST LOVE

"He smiles at me, and I am suddenly seventeen again...
the year I realize that love doesn't follow the rules,
the year I understood that nothing is worth having
so much as something unattainable"
Jodi Picoult

I love New York but it can be a lonely city. When I think of all
the millions of small apartments inhabited by singles longing for love,
I am mind-boggled. But despite the fact that I had never had a terribly
long-term relationship, I suspect there was always a romantic in me
just waiting for the right guy. And the right guy for my romantic heart
finally came into my life. When you least expect it, things can change.
The light finds a way to enter, doesn't it?

Through many of my years in New York, once I had joined The
American Mime Theatre, I worked in the evenings. This was typical
for New York actors who were in-between shows. Of course, most
waiters in New York are actors waiting around for their break. I remember trying my hand at restaurant work and just didn't have it in
me. I honestly think I'd have done better to own my own restaurant
and create the dishes and the interior design. But being a waiter
requires a very different kind of mentality. My dilemma was that all I
really wanted was to support myself while dedicating my life to the
mime theater, and since that was the priority, I'd be forced to take a
menial job with minimal pay. Sometimes being stuck between a rock
and hard place comes with the territory of one choice or the other. If
Nicheron-Shoshu had taught me something, it was that life was cause
and effect. The mystic law went deeper than that I'm sure, but I wasn't

92

seeing that just yet. I took the jobs I could get. I worked a couple of days a week as a receptionist for a psycho-pharmacologist, meeting several celebrities, in fact, with mental disorders or drug addictions of all sorts. That too seemed to come with the territory, as if being right-brained precluded sanity.

Anyway, in the evenings, I sang in Japanese piano bars. There were several of these odd sort-of Karaoke piano bars throughout New York, as the Japanese community was quite large. I think they were a contemporary version of Geisha houses and appeased something in their culture that evidently still exists. The businessmen gathered in the evenings to drink and often get drunk with their associates while being catered to by lovely hostesses. I found my way into this bizarre business that allowed me to live my life without becoming a slaving waitress. I also had a couple of freelance businesses that I had running ads in the papers for. These jobs offered me a little autonomy. This was one... I was a lady interior house painter for years. Yes, I was delicate and certainly didn't look the part, but I hauled heavy ladders and painted my way through New York City for years.

The most consistent paycheck, however came from the Japanese bar scene. I was silent during my days doing mime or co-authoring non-speaking theatre pieces, while my evenings brought me to a very different culture, indeed a very different world. Later I found out that Cyndi Lauper had actually worked these clubs and sang in them as well. Most people don't know about this underground life, but it still exists today.

My life was certainly busy though by now I was longing for love. The only men I knew however were my brothers from the mime theatre, or the married men who frequented the Japanese nightclubs. The flirting over cocktails was a turnoff to be quite honest. And though dressing up in evening gowns was "fun" for a while, it just all seemed inauthentic somehow. at least for me... this night life fulfilled a need from a culture I ultimately didn't understand. And I'd rather not examine too harshly but I'll say this; it didn't fit in with my image of feminine power... plain and simple...

I worked in these bars for a few years and because of what they became to me, I never suspected that I would actually meet a great love of my life there. But I did meet someone. And I have to admit it, it was love at first sight. It literally fulfilled every notion old love stories had taught me about romance... The only problem was that many of those beautiful tales ended in tragedy. (as if tragedy was inherent in love) This relationship sent me to the moon and the stars, but ultimately did not work out and perhaps was never meant to. I was ready for love, but perhaps only ready for the feeling of it... and for the kind of romance that only comes with clandestine relationships. Sometimes these are the ones you can throw yourself into with abandonment and not ever lose the spark over time. I never lost my adoration for this man who had been the first love of my life. Of course, I was a late bloomer, but who wouldn't be with such a childhood? It was an amazing phenomenon at all that I could ever feel this way, but I did. And I felt it for ten full years through thick and thin and through long, long distances. We always thought our love was like the movie "Same Time Next Year", though it never continued after I'd met my future husband. I still think of him though, and I thank him for his loving.

His name was Joe. I remember being drawn to his unusual look. He was an interesting mix of American Indian, Chinese, and Irish. And of course, with my European mix, we may have appeared opposites, but we made up the world... I liked that. Joe was beautiful in every way, though a little mysterious. Maybe I needed a little mystery to throw some of my own dreamy romance onto. Whatever it was, I held him in my heart through all those years. I still have his image stuck in my mind of the first time we'd encountered each other. I'd come in late to work that night; I almost stayed home in fact. In any event, it was a bustling evening, music was playing and all the tables were full. I remember after putting my coat away, I started into the main room and for whatever reason, stopped for a moment and I glanced at the bar. I think it was instinct that called me over. Who knows? Instinct had called me before, God knows.

I didn't think much of it, but suddenly was struck by a most unusual feeling. There was an energy calling, that's all I knew. I turned around and realized someone had been staring at me... and once I saw who it was, I felt utterly trapped by his gaze. That's the truth. It was like that. We were total strangers, but our eyes locked into each other's and couldn't break away without a good deal of willpower. It was the oddest thing I'd ever experienced with the exception of the time I had encountered my own soul while tripping. Yes, I'd say this was a bit like entering an altered state. When we came to our senses he just said, "You're beautiful"... and I found myself responding with the same: "You are too".

I think it was the manager who finally interrupted and told me to get to work. As I recall, I could barely get through the evening. I simply couldn't forget him, and felt the most horrible remorse for having felt this uncanny attraction for one minute only to have it taken away from me without a hope of finding him again. The evening came to a close at around 1:30 a.m. Yes, when most were fast asleep, we were just closing shop and often would go out to all-night sushi bars or even to the Korean version. This night I was more than ready to go home. I collected my coat and started for the door. And there, waiting to open it for me was Joe. He had returned for me. He'd apparently been thinking of me too through the night. I guess our attraction was just too strong to dismiss. Sometimes things are inevitable; this was.

I remember not saying much. The silence between us was ever so much more loaded than anything we might have said. That evening began our long-distance love affair, and my heart remained faithful to him despite various boyfriends that I'd had over the years. Joe was my romance and no one could compare. He was the most beautiful for sure, and beauty had always taken me with its spirit and its poetry. I know women rarely think of men in such terms, but I guess there was something about him that elicited my admiration, and perhaps it was because he was so different... And I liked that.

There was so much about him that almost seemed to demand my heart in a way that I'd never known before. But when I look back to decipher why, I tend to think that it was because he dared to look at me from his soul. He dared to connect unlike anyone ever had. Maybe that's the beauty of such a relationship that never has a chance to be soiled by the interruption of life. Maybe the annoying conflicts of day-to-day routines would have wounded that initial connection, but honestly, no one had ever engendered my attention quite like that, or to such a degree. And certainly, such soul-to-soul contact is a rare and precious thing, and because of it, he made me feel completely treasured.

Joe had led such a different life, and though he had a genuinely gentle way about him, I suspect he was attracted to a bit of danger. I could never quite fathom this quiet, sweet man in a boxing ring, but he apparently boxed his way through his military days. He was also engaged in demolition derbies, which simply seemed unfathomable to me. I'd envisioned men with such passions as rather macho and as such unrelatable to the likes of me. But Joe was put together in the most unique way. He was a rarity. He was a gentle, romantic and vulnerable man, yet had a power. Maybe this was my strange makeup as well, and possibly between the two of us, there was an element of danger that fueled our relationship. In any event, it lasted for the longest time, but it couldn't go on forever.

I wish sometimes that I could see him again. I think of him often. But we had our time and place and indeed our purpose in each other's lives. It's quite possible that I grew more into my womanhood because of his presence in my life, as things I'd never known existed in me began to emerge. In many ways Joe made me ready for more than I'd even imagined; the possibility of marriage.

I wonder though, when I hear women speak of the long-lost loves of their youth, they've evidently kept alive through the years. The story is not terribly unique as it happens... Perhaps long-lost love fits the profile of some archetypal lover who can remain intact when we've grown old... well beyond the age of romance. Perhaps there's an eternal Romeo and Juliet within many of us... and even thinking of them holds the peculiar feeling of youth and vibrancy... I don't know though I find the notion intriguing...

Despite it all, it was clear at the time that Joe and I were not meant to be, despite our soul connection. But at least now I knew that it was possible to open my heart and let a man into my life and I was going to do what was necessary to make that happen.

METAPHYSICS & SPIRITUALITY

"A Sacred wandering awakens you.
It connects you to your "authentic self".
It can empower you to find your voice, To enlarge your vision,
To nurture your Soul. To create healthy boundaries.
To bravely try something new."
Dana Arcuri

Many things happen over a span of time and my life was always chockfull. It becomes impossible to notate it all. A life in retrospect seems like a few broad strokes connecting some details, but when you look back with a certain lens, one's life begins to look like a piece of artwork. Maybe it's because I'm an artist that I think this way. Or maybe it's because the mystery of all life is creative and each one of us on our path, without really knowing it, is engaged in a creative process. We can consciously steer a bit of that process or not.

I had claimed early on that I wanted to attain enlightenment through this lifetime, and though I had stumbled upon higher states of consciousness, I hardly knew what true enlightenment was. I certainly had psychic experiences from early on, but I had never seriously explored the arena. My work in the performing arts, however, gave me great insight into the human condition and spirit. Without formal study of psychology or even philosophy, I delved into the work of archetypes and symbols while writing mythic theatre. Almost by accident I was touching upon a psychic realm of sorts, and of course the door had been opened since childhood. Soon I would dive head-on into the world of psychic phenomena and turn down the road of my journey once again.

The mystic law of cause and effect might have been at work with my own destiny right around this time. There had been a new group of students coming down from Pennsylvania to study with Paul. They actually had a small performing arts company themselves called "Touchstone" and though they knew some mime, they did speaking theatre as well. Clearly there was much to learn from our discipline. And for anyone in these kinds of performing arts, this training was invaluable. A division of "Touchstone" was their perfectly delightful children's theatre and with the onset of American Mime training, they decided to try their hand at a non-speaking children's piece. And they approached me with a proposal to direct them. It would mean coming up to Bethlehem, Pennsylvania for a while, but I gladly accepted. Actually, it was a great getaway.

I was being commissioned to direct them through the process of building a new piece. These kinds of companies are really unusual in their collaborative effort. Hopefully through a shared language, a truly magical result can come of such a process. I was used to theatre for more sophisticated audiences, but we put our heads together and wound up with a terrific little piece called "The Comic Book Kid". It was a morality tale of sorts about superheroes, good and evil, and learning the proper usage of one's power in this world. "The Comic Book Kid" may not have been Noble Peace Prize worthy, but our hearts were in the right place. And when all was said and done, I'd made some special friends that would remain so for a long time after.

The intriguing thing about that whole experience was how it seemed the precursor to some very deep spiritual work with crystal healing of my own. Synchronistically or otherwise, the symbol that I had given our young superhero in the children's tale was an enormous power wand made of pure crystal. I'd known nothing of crystal healing at that time, at least consciously, but soon I would find my way to it as if it was meant to be.

Soon after the completion of my work in Pennsylvania I returned to Manhattan. These days I had been palling around with a couple of "Touchstone" and Mime Theatre friends. It often seemed that I had tribes of friends to experience new adventures with. This night I was with my dear friends, Lorraine, Janet and Tim. Once again, something in the air seemed to call me and so I answered, this time with a tribe of friends equally willing to heed the call.

It might have seemed aimless as we wandered down the street but a flickering candlelight through a store front window caught our attention. And it changed my life forever. It was so inviting somehow that there was no way to pass it by. I remember our four faces pressed against the window like kids at a candy shop. What we saw inside was definitely mystical in nature, maybe a little frightening, but absolutely intriguing.

I remember someone coming to the door and inviting us in. We just looked at each other with mouths gaping. Should we go in? I mean it looked a little like we were entering a witch's cauldron or a weird cult of some sort. And yet we found ourselves saying, "All right, sure". We could only pray that all would be well and that we wouldn't be thrown into some big oven like Hansel and Gretel. It was a little strange, and got even stranger. We needed a little faith, but then it was faith that brought us there in the first place.

There was a large circle of folks sitting cross-legged. Talk about tribal. The lights were dimmed and you could see only by candlelight. No one spoke for the longest time. The young woman who had let us in very quietly gave us each a small crystal and sat us down in the circle. I remember the four of us darted our eyes around the circle and back again to each other giggling like children. There was silence for a while longer when suddenly this one young man began to speak. He was mesmerizing. With the light casting its shadow the way it did, there seemed to be something almost unearthly about him. He was an unusually beautiful man with piercing blue eyes that stared straight ahead into dimensions he'd soon bring us into.

For the next 40 minutes, that young man took us through a guided meditation that was utterly transcendental. When we came back to earth, I think a little of me was left in the ethers, but I was completely fascinated by the whole experience. That night began years worth of adventures into the spirit world and into further development of my soul's journey. The young man's name was Alan Davidson and he had led crystal healing meditations once a week, along with in-depth sessions of all sorts running the full gamut of spiritual exploration.

There's so much more to life than meets the eye of course, but it seemed uncanny to me that I had just written a children's play about the power of crystals and now, by complete accident, I was so thrown into its magical, mysterious world. But was it an accident? No, it was not. Nothing was an accident ever, and the dynamics of my life would reveal that truth forevermore. These days I call myself a "synchronicity queen". Those who know me well think I'm a mystic living a life in suburban America, but a mystic nevertheless. It's true my veil seems to be thin, for better or for worse. But for someone who claimed she wanted enlightenment this lifetime, these sessions were perfect. I obviously was blessed to stumble upon this storefront with all the metaphysical training it led me to for years to come. Such training would cost thousands today and would all have been under the umbrella of a kind of college for spiritual arts.

I had past life regressions, spiritual adjustments and channeling sessions with masters of all sorts. In fact, I recall one who had "remembered" me from the Himalayas. I did rebirthings, neural linguistic reprogramming, inner child work, and deep, deep work with the unconscious where all my childhood wounds still lay waiting to be tended. I had healings and I learned to heal. And I was shifting for certain as my veil got thinner and thinner. I'll never forget the aftereffects of some of my sessions. They so often were about the light.

I had a dream during this time so psychically powerful I just can't forget it. I was with David Bowie of all people, on another planet (perhaps not so far from the truth). The imagery in the dream was like a camera at close-up slowly panning out to reveal the larger picture.

> David and I were together in a deep cave of sorts. We were apparently very much at home there and quite comfortable with each other. The camera spanned back a little when all at once a beam of light shined down upon us from above. It was as bright as could be. The view spanned even further back till our image was infinitesimal, while the cave itself was enormous. The light beam came through a small opening from above, and what was revealed beyond the opening was the cosmos itself. The image was awesome but not merely because of the visual aspect; it was auditory as well. There was a building crescendo of sorts and by the end of the dream, the words "Rock Star" came through — Wow!

I must say, there was often a kind of a glory and grace to some of the dreams I had at that time, and my dreams were becoming more and more clairvoyant. I was having so many fascinating experiences, and I felt ready for them unlike years before when I'd had visitations from my mother. But there was an experience I'll never forget that scared the heck out of me and I still am disturbed by it.

I came home late from one of my sessions with Alan. He had done an adjustment; a spiritual adjustment on me. Hard to describe except to say that with a layout of crystals up and down my body, I fell into a deeply altered state while Alan laid hands for at least 40 minutes. There was no doubt about it – Alan had a remarkable power, but so did I. I'm not sure what happened that night, but between the power of the healer, the "healee", and the universe above, something within me was forever changed. He called it a "spiritual shift." It was a spiritual shift all right, but if I had easy access to the collective mind before this, then the boundaries now were being torn away completely. In any event, I was told to go home after my "shift," drink lots of water and get a good night's sleep… and observe.

Sleep was no problem, that's for certain. I was exhausted after this experience, so when I went to sleep that night I practically fell into a stupor; I slept like a rock. And that's why it seemed so odd to wake up in the middle of the night, but I did. And as I opened my eyes, I simply could not believe the vision before me. Three beams of light stood in the middle of my room as clear as clear could be, and carried a palpable energy with them. I tell you, it was right out of a sci-fi movie, and it frightened me so much that I could only hide under my blankets like a 2-year-old. In fact, the only time that I remembered such fear was the night that I had seen the faces of Jesus and the Devil float by my window so long ago. What had I opened the gateway to through my spiritual shift? Good Lord, was I hallucinating? I'll never know what forces I had brushed shoulders with that evening, but I could not have this sort of thing in my life, and so I yelled out from beneath my covers: "Go away! I'm not ready for you! I don't know what you want from me, but I don't want you here!"

I remember I had a large crystal by my bedside and so I grabbed it and I pulled it under the covers with me and held it tight to my heart through the night. When I woke up in the morning, all was well. Life was surely a mystery, but interestingly enough I think there was something almost being played out in my own life that had merely been alluded to in that little mime play that I'd written with Touchstone. Maybe I was the Comic Book Kid. Maybe I was the Comic Book Kid, learning the lessons of crystal power, but more importantly the power of the universe.

In any event, I may have warded off my visions that night, but I went forward with my studies through the years without fear. And I had many remarkable experiences. There was work with totems, guides, and a little with the archetypes that I'd already been exploring.

I'll never forget a most wonderful creative visualization that came up in Technicolor one night. I think this revealed my "inner wise woman". I saw the image of myself peering into a crystal ball. On my shoulder stood an owl and a wolf was by my side. Inside the crystal ball that I was looking through, the very same image was duplicated, and then into the next crystal ball again, and again, and then again, and again, and again, and again, and it would obviously go on forever. Maybe my initial fascination with infinity had remained within me and was here to stay. Maybe my mother had brought to me the notion of eternity and it now was my chance to get a stronger glimpse of it.

We started working with the I Ching and Tarot, which I took up years later but merely toyed with in these days. I remember the cards that kept coming up were the moon and the death card. I was told not to consider these literally, though I already knew I was a moon child and death had hit me early on. It was, however, explained to me that the death card actually meant birth, the birth of new ideas and shifting paradigms. Nothing could have been truer. My spiritual adventure had brought me to a much, much higher degree of consciousness and even of a stronger relationship to the universal soul, the one I have come to call The Great Creator.

I was definitely in a state of grace and held on to it for a very, very long time. My spiritual journey that year was sped up in a very profound way, but perhaps the most important byproduct of all of this work wasn't simply a further opening of my third eye, but the opening of my heart. Of course, I'd known a beautiful romance and love with Joe, but unlike the tragic endings in all of those Bette Davis films, I really did want more than the moon and the stars. I wanted a real man, a real relationship, even if it meant I would have to work hard to keep it alive. And I wanted more than anything to have children. The days of choosing theatre over family were long gone. With a little bit of growing up, some priorities do change.

There was one meditation that I had that seemed to allude to that fact.

I went within and there I saw the image of a young boy. Again, like a camera, my mind's eye scanned him slowly as he became clearer and clearer. He had long, silky, thick brown hair with brown eyes; his face was beautiful. My vision swirled around him as he floated in a womblike position, though he was not an infant. There was such a feeling of love and radiance and I just wanted to embrace that child. When I described my image to the group, I told them that I believed he was my son, and he was the reason I had come into this lifetime. That was quite a statement coming from me.

I knew there was something to this. Maybe the greatest bonds of all are between mother and child. This I already knew to be the case with my mother. Perhaps one day I would know such a bond from the other side of that relationship. Perhaps one day I would have a son and I would know a soul bond like no other. And perhaps he was the one that I came to this lifetime for.

What I did feel to be the case was a certain compassion through all my spiritual work that would bring the world to me in ways that I had not truly known before. My future husband was waiting for me and was just around the bend and I would meet him soon.

It was 1985 and I was about to turn 33-years-old. I remember thinking that I had finally reached my prime and had come into womanhood. Some people have an ideal age they hold within forever; 33 was mine. Life was not only harmonious, but vital on so many levels, and I tend to think that the meditations and healing work that I was now practicing on a daily basis had put me in God's grace. And so, at 33, the Universe seemed to shed its light on me.

By now I'd pretty much moved out of the nightclub scene into what was known as the "party scene", a growing industry that provided entertainment to corporations and private events. The "new vaudeville," utilized the talents of jugglers, circus artists, performance artists, dancers, mimes, magicians, character actors, and more. I have no idea how long it had been around, but I fell into it almost by accident when I put an ad in the New Yorker Magazine as "mime for rent." Really, it was on a complete whim to do such a thing, but it didn't take much effort and seemed to pay off well. I got responses and began designing tailor-made mime pieces for weddings and events.

I approached it however, as a solo artist and honestly, never knew how big a deal the corporate entertainment business actually was. Since I had little contact with other kinds of talent, it didn't occur to me to expand upon the business. But my friend, Janet, did. It was funny to me because I never would have thought I would see her as a successful businesswoman, but she took this town by storm. Janet had chutzpa and a business savvy that I didn't. And she had contact with talent of all sorts, having been a part of the Renaissance Festival in upstate New York.

In any event, with the advent of her "Entertainment connection", I started to make a little money in the performing arts for the first time. One thing led to the next and quickly I built skills I'd not even known I had a gift for. (like costume design and floral arrangements) By 1985 I was able to leave the bar scene and earn a living solely through the arts.

They say it's not easy to change your life despite the inherit desire for more, whatever that means. What I do know, however, is that action is magic. And perhaps my daily spiritual rituals had "magically" manifested possibilities that I hadn't specifically anticipated. The doors to abundance were opening up and 1985 would open up much more.

I was about to turn 33 and interestingly enough, so were quite a few of my friends. We were all Scorpios and decided this year to share the celebration. It was a great one – my first birthday party since my childhood with Mady. A big bash was thrown at Janet's company loft and we invited everyone we knew.

Something was definitely in the air yet I hadn't put too much credence into the psychic reading that I had been given that very morning as a birthday gift. The psychic had told me I was going to meet my future husband soon. I remember feeling a kind of thrill when he told me this, but had put it out of my head by now. It was only later that I realized how true and how soon all of that would come to pass... that very night, in fact.

Well, as if out of a dream he appeared. And honestly, I knew. I knew who he was. Life can be surreal; it was that night. The lights were dimmed for the party. But I recall seeing his image at the door as he entered. And though I'm quite near-sighted I was struck by his image. Maybe it was his aura that got me.

He does have a certain charisma; I have to admit. But whatever it was that I saw in him, he obviously saw it in me too.

It's so strange how these things work. This complete stranger made his way through the crowd without hesitation and came right up to me that night, and I swear I knew I was going to marry him. I had loved my Joe for ten years now, and no one could take that away from me... yet somehow, I'd opened room enough for a new love and I was meeting him this night. The next day I wrote a poem about him and this is how it went.

"A Brief Encounter." November 1985

1985 two strangers meet and the world fades away as they search each other's eyes. It's as if they stand alone in a force field for one brief moment. Then a voice breaks the trance and they part in denial of their strange recognition. Those eyes might have embraced each other's centuries before, but what might come to pass now will never be known, for we dare not think beyond our own paradigm, and we dare not believe that two strangers could possibly have been in love long before they met in 1985. And so, they go their separate ways and they may think of each other now and then. But soon the memory fades. And dare I muse? If they should meet again tomorrow or in the year 3000, will they live the moment again and find its worth?

I didn't know how it would all play out, and yet I knew. I always knew he was the one. Whether the timing was right for us or not, I knew that we would wind up marrying. I remember the French film by Claude La Louche that had made such an impact on me about how souls are destined to find a way to each other despite obstacles. They may pass each other in the streets, just miss their "proper meeting" by seconds, and it may even take lifetimes. But if there's destiny to it, they will surely meet. This film was called "Et Maintenant" (And Now My Love). I always felt this kind of spiritual romance about life itself. Naturally I'd feel it about love. I had this feeling about Paul. It was only a matter of time. Anyway, Janet had made arrangements for the two of us to "gig" together. As I recall, we had some really wild early adventures together as a result. Paul did a little mime; some juggling and other skills thank God, because our first job together would have been horrifying had he not had his bag of tricks with him this night. We had been hired to meet and greet a small party at a Jewish event out of town somewhere. This would be a cinch. We had costumes and mime skills ready to go. And with an easy-going train ride to Connecticut, the evening was looking more and more like a date than work. However, we got the shock of our lives when we arrived to discover that there was no one to meet because the guests were already seated and waiting for an actual show. Oh my God, a show! We had no show. It was the wildest pickle I had ever found myself in.

After eight minutes of trotting out aimless robotic mime skills, we had to get off the stage and figure something out quickly. It was a terrifying moment... Even the best improv artists would have panicked, but somehow, we pulled it off. I think I quickly talked Paul through a little American Mime play called "The Scarecrow" and the rest I left in Paul's hands. I have to say I was awestruck by his resourcefulness. He exhibited a kind of brilliance I'm not sure I'd seen before. And I found it exceedingly attractive... And I was struck by the way he handled that audience. Did we pull it off? They loved us! I seem to recall getting a standing ovation.

What a first date – I was smitten, and so was he. Even so, however, our love affair was destined to move forward in fits and starts with long absences because, as taken as he was with me, he was unfortunately "taken" by someone else. He was in a relationship and he was trying hard to be faithful. I remember feeling very much like the pursuer back then, but I simply couldn't help my conviction that against all odds, he was somehow part of my destiny. I'd worked hard to draw into my life the very soul I was meant to be with. And sentimental or not, I felt it was he. Flawed or not, I felt it was he. He was quite different than anyone that I had found myself attracted to before. But I had the uncanny feeling we were two souls who had known each other forever, and would know each other again. But I had to let him go for now. I had not been ready for a full commitment before this, but he was obviously not ready for me, and so I let him go.

Perhaps it's the hardest lesson of all; there's just so much we can control. People come into our lives and they go. They live and they die. And though I myself have had a psychic sense of things from the start, the mystery of life is full of surprises and sometimes we just have to surrender.

It was a year I will never forget. I had been touched by spirit, of course, but sadly I'd have to give up on the love I was so certain of... I suppose in a way you could have called the ending of my relationship with Paul a kind of stillbirth. I remember feeling that way early on, at least for a while. I did a lot of writing during that time, as poetry seemed to heal my heart. And I was quite prolific as I recall. I remember putting an entire book together. That's what comes of lost love. This was my way to "sing the blues." And the blues helped me through my apparent loss. I was able to release my heartache and my concern at that time. What was to be would be in the hands of the Divine, and the hands of time.

There were other losses around that same time... real ones that were heartbreaking. You don't expect death before one's time. Of course, it's naïve to think in such terms as "one's time", but honestly, when someone young and seemingly strong dies it's simply hard to fathom, and it's hard to bear. I'm thinking now of my dear friend Kevin Kaloostian.

I remember him well. He was striking with his thick, black eyebrows and near-white hair. He was 40 years old when he died. Kevin was one of my "brothers" from the mime theatre... We'd worked together for years...

His loss was hard on all of us, but I've always been left with an eerie feeling about it, as if death had paid him a visit one day and decided that our Kevin was just right for the pickin', and whisked him away in one month's time. It was that crazy. He was with us one day and gone the next from a vicious pancreatic cancer, and that was that. It simply stunned all of us. I always wonder though if something was actually at work beyond the disease, something in the air so to speak, perhaps a force unknown to us. I know it sounds cryptic, but a most peculiar thing happened around that time that I have never shaken.

I've known of psychic forces before; this seemed particularly supernatural. Shortly before Kevin had taken ill, we'd gone into rehearsal on a playwriting grant. It had been some time since we had written one together. Through this collaboration we decided to put together a piece with the working title, "Spirituality", and Kevin was the lead. It was actually going quite well, but the project was chucked after he died; I think we all agreed that it would just be too painful to see someone else in the role. But more than that, there was an unspoken contract that we had made after we'd witnessed something so bizarre that no one could discuss it.

I'll explain this way... As I'd said before, the name of the piece we'd been working on was called, "Spirituality"... Well, as it happened, it stylistically unfolded scene by scene into a series of spiritual snapshots, if you will, and was really quite abstract in nature... You'll just have to imagine that we had indeed captured some essence of spirit in this little work in progress, and it was starting to look like a work of art. One day, Paul brought his camera into rehearsal and shot a few rolls of film. We were all anxious to see the results, but that film once exposed, sat for a while once we became aware of Kevin's cancer. We would get to view these photos after his death.

When the time seemed appropriate, we finally gathered to view the photos. We were excited to see how we had captured him in his leading role. He never got to perform "Spirituality" but we'd at least have something left of his months of hard work and artistry... But, when we opened the package and viewed what had been shot that day, photo after photo revealed the most peculiar thing that I have ever seen. In each shot of Kevin, his image was skewed with long streaks of colors and light. Everyone else was intact, but Kevin's image was not. He seemed morphed into light. It's hard to express. And if something had gone haywire in the processing, why then was it only his image that looked this way?

It was actually frightening and without saying a word, Paul quickly packed away the photos and we never spoke of it again. I've seen many strange things in my time. This was one... This was remarkable, perhaps as surreal in the same way as the three beams of light I'd seen those years ago, or the encounters I'd had with the spirit of my own mother... But what I am privy to, through all these experiences, is that the nature of reality is indeed eternal, and the distinction between such things as life and death is perhaps an illusion... or at least multidimensional. It may be frightening, but really, it's very beautiful when all is said and done. In truth life is beautiful and its mystery is infinite.

In any event, I was glad that I had gone to see Kevin in his last days. I needed to say goodbye, but felt a sense of relief when he himself told me that he was completely reconciled and at peace. This was the dream that I had when he died.

In my dream I walked side-by-side with my friend who died three nights ago. Split by a line, I stood on the soil of life and he on the soil of death. We spoke in some unearthly fashion and I wept, pleading with him to return to the light of day. I was wretched with remorse and somehow, he managed to pass his hand through the threshold and took hold of mine. I squeezed his hand with all my might and felt his presence. I felt his presence beyond the illusion of my false perceptions of life and death, beyond my dreams. I felt his touch, so intensely tangible, perhaps more tangible than when he was alive just three days ago. Oh God... through separate dimensions love reaches out and in that I am forever blessed.

I had lost so many. By that time there had been others: my mother, my mother's mother, Papa Sam, my paternal grandparents, and now Kevin. I always felt the Angel of Death was sitting upon my shoulder and because of it, my view of life was quite profound. It put me on an edge somehow, a constant reminder to celebrate life, to color it vibrantly. I do happen to believe somehow in reincarnation, but I always loved that phrase nevertheless that goes like this: "Get it right the first time. This is not a rehearsal. Live your life." Live your life!

So many traumatic events had happened that year despite my hard work and even feeling that I had been in God's grace. I came to realize that no matter how you try, you cannot keep life at bay. Along with living it fully, all experience is invited in for good reason.

I had one more loss that year that I will never forget. I've always loved my pets and never lived without one. I had my little black cat for 16 years and though I had detained the inevitable with the laying of hands many times before, it was time for her to go.

There is a story here I don't always like revisiting because it's one that I carry a good deal of guilt over and I regret. To tell the tale I have to go back in time, a little before Kevin's death and even before meeting Paul Borrillo. This would bring us somewhere around July of '85. I had lived in several apartments through New York but now I was comfortably settled in my Gramercy Park studio. On the heels of all my spiritual work, however, I knew that something had to change, and sometimes the literal act of moving can set new energy in motion. Perhaps I was tampering with fate. But I honestly thought that my idea of moving in with my old friend Sho-Chan was a move in the right direction. It was daring in a way, but it came from a genuine attempt to deepen our relationship.

We had been great friends for so long, and since neither of us had ever made a commitment to anyone really, we foolishly thought we could transform our platonic "love affair" into a romantic one... I wouldn't recommend this sort of venture to any young person. It backfired with us in the horrible way. Sho's affection for me was strong enough, to eventually turn me around or so I thought. Our hearts were in the right place, I suppose, but these things rarely work out. How sad to look back at the way it all ended when it began so innocently and full of hope.

I sublet my apartment and moved in with my little cat to Sho's loft between Little Italy, Soho and Chinatown. In the beginning we enjoyed the experiment. We decorated together, cooked gourmet foods together, and played house well for a while. In many ways it seemed it would work out, but I guess it was naïve because the newness of our adventure eventually wore off and discomfort set in along with a pressure to "fall in love." And unfortunately, the easygoing nature of our friendship was slipping away as a result. I guess that's the risk you take when you tinker with fate.

It was becoming more than obvious that it wasn't meant to be and that if we were to save any remnant of our friendship, I'd better leave soon. It had become painful for both of us, but what I couldn't fathom was how Sho put himself in a state of denial about what was happening. He seemed to swallow the whole obvious truth despite the obvious. I don't understand this "thing" in people, men mostly, who believe it's better to bury the truth rather than to discuss it. Conflicts hidden away in the dark depths brew, and they brew into beasts. I felt this was happening, but couldn't anticipate how it would emerge or when. I only knew that I was going to have to take control and let him know that I would be leaving. What would play out would have to in its own way. We took a risk and what would be, would be.

So, fast forward... it was now November as I return to the story of my 33rd birthday in 1985. That morning I went to the Tarot reading that my friend had given me as a gift. The psychic told me that I would be meeting my future husband soon. That night I met him at the Scorpio birthday party my friend's and I shared at Janet Lee's loft. We had a brief encounter, but I knew that he was the one. I went home that night and was more reconciled than ever that I would simply have to end it with Sho. I would do so tomorrow evening, come hell or high water.

In the morning when I woke, I sat down and I wrote a poem that I would call "The Brief Encounter." Whether I knew it or not, I certainly felt I had met my husband.

And then the evening came and I bucked up for a necessary confrontation. But, before I could even think to confront him, Sho Chan surprised me with yet another birthday party. Oh, my Lord, what timing! He had arranged everything and honestly, it was just too beautiful to bear. My 33rd birthday, the year that I love the most, practically tore me in pieces that night. Sho-chan hosted my party with such visible joy and pride. It was almost horrifying to have been given this extraordinary gift knowing what was to come. But it had to end, and it did that night.

It all came out when the party ended and the guests went home. No doubt our darkest experiences have purpose but nonetheless I could have done without this one… My dear old friend went insane. I never had seen this side of him but it came out like a kundalini force… Certainly, there had been no sign of a violent trait in him before, but this evening he brought it forth and I almost lost my life because of it. He lunged at me like an animal, threw his hands around my neck and began to strangle me. I remember feeling completely overtaken, but I fought for my life. It was a horrific scene and God Almighty, I never saw it coming; not this! But in the middle of it all, I remember the confusion that came over his face. It was almost as if the "real" Sho had left his own body and came back just in time to release me. Good Lord. He fell back onto the carpet in remorse as I caught my breath. I couldn't believe what had happened. And though he begged me to forgive him, I'd gotten the chill of my life and just had to get the hell out of there.

That old terrible feeling of wanting to run came back to me all at once, to run like the wind. Again, the notion of freedom was all that mattered to me, and though I really had a deep fondness for that man, it was over. As sure as day, it was over. I called my friend Charna and moved in with her till my sublet was up for the month. I had my stuff hauled out of his loft and a friend came to get my poor cat who had been witness to it all. It was a horrible event and it's amazing to me how we ever heal from the traumatic force of violence. But I guess the spirit can be indelible as they say.

I never saw Sho-Chan again, though years later I tried to contact him for some kind of loving resolution, but I couldn't track him down. I still wish for that with all my heart. The saddest thing of all was what came of that ill-fated evening just two nights after. My friend Dale called me with the news. He had taken my cat Piewacket when I couldn't because Charna had two cats of her own. It kills me to think of what my beloved kitty had gone through with all these fierce experiences and moves, and now she had to buck up and move into some stranger's house in Brooklyn. We never think how much our pets may need their master, but the bond we had, had been a long one with a lot of love. Dale told me Pie had gone into a coma and he had her at an all-night veterinarian hospital. I came as fast as I could, but there was no saving her. The vet was just waiting for me to sign papers. I'll never forget how she lay there so pathetically. But the most pathetic thing about it all was that they couldn't successfully euthanize her because her veins had collapsed from weakness. Perhaps she would have died within the next few nights, perhaps the next hour, but what does one do with a dying cat and nowhere to bring her? They told me to rouse her enough to get her blood circulating and with tears I called her name. I kept calling, getting louder and louder and louder till she came to for one brief moment as if to say goodbye. And they shot the killing drug into her veins that put her to sleep.

I was beside myself. I became hysterical. I think that I cried for her the tears that I had held in for everyone in my life that I had ever loved who now had passed. It's funny how that happens, and it seems to be a fairly common story. Mine was only made more intense because of the circumstances, but I think I cried too in mourning for Sho and for whatever had died in me. Our beloved pets are the ones who seem to open the watershed of our hearts when we have shut ourselves off from mankind. Why? It's always intrigued me. Anyway, Piewacket's passing brought the tears of the world to my eyes and I will never forget her, and I can't forget Sho.

I lived with Charna for a few months as I recall. I had my affair with Paul by now, and eventually had put it to rest. I said my goodbyes to my dear friend Kevin and I returned to my studio in Gramercy. With all that had happened in just a matter of a couple of months, there was so much to process that some quiet time felt just right. That with the help of Alan Davidson, I went on with my spiritual work. I remember the day we pulled out the Tarot and that death card turned up. Nothing could have been more accurate. These months had brought with them so many endings and even more would come with friends who'd contracted AIDS. I knew as well that it was just a matter of time before my father would pass on, as he already had been struggling with cancer. It seemed to all come at once like some kind of personal Armageddon, but indeed as Alan had explained, death often brings with it an uncanny birth of new possibility to one's life… And after all, death is the Grim Reaper and the Grim Reaper is a harvester of that which lives quite "fruitfully". It's difficult to imagine at times, but life does go on.

Things change and when you least expect it, the light will indeed reenter. My life had always proved this to be so. Maybe it was a belief system that I had created for myself or maybe a warrior's spirit within me. But despite the intense nature of my journey, nothing could keep me down for very long, nothing. And I knew others whose lives looked like cotton candy compared to mine, yet they had become depressives or alcoholics or worse, had committed suicide. I'm not sure if it's brain chemistry or one's outlook, but even before I tallied it, I think I believed that life was essentially beautiful.

I remember the Japanese tale of Rashomon that described a tragic incident in the forest retold by the three who had been involved. It's a brilliant story. The experience of each person was entirely different, but the facts were the same. It was a different tale for each. Life is like that; it's like Rashomon. To me it's all beautiful somehow, almost poetic. One of my favorite lines from a Williams' play that I had done always seemed quintessential to me: "We live in a world of light and shadow, but the shadow is almost as luminous as the light." I don't know how many actually feel this way. Most place judgment onto their experiences and the whole notion of the darkness seems to bring up fear or feelings of negativity as if any one side of life could be separated from the other; as if living in the light meant the shadow was evil. What a gross misconception I always thought. In any event, through my spiritual work I have to admit in many ways, I was seeing more and more of the light. Certainly, out of the shadow of so much death, the light was long overdue, and when it came back into my life, it brought with it a whole new world. Yes, it was a time of new beginnings. Alan was right.

A LITTLE DESTINY

"A Soulmate is not found. A Soulmate is recognized."
Vironika Tugaleva

It was summertime and like many balmy evenings in Manhattan, the pubs and outdoor cafes were filled with friends meeting friends. New York is so alive when a little warmth fills the air. This evening called me out, and so my roommate and I decided to go to St. Mark's Place for a bite. At the time there was a wonderful restaurant down there called Do-Joes. People would line up to get in because the fusion food was so good, but also so reasonably priced. It was one of my favorites, and evidently many people felt the same. It's a big city and very dense, but some places seem to be like magnets bringing together old friends and new. I think Do-Joes must have been a little like that, but even so I wouldn't have guessed I would see anyone that I knew there that night, particularly someone that I had worked so hard to forget. But there he was, as bright as a star, beaming at me with so much warmth that I couldn't help but melt.

Paul had come back into my life that night and the charisma that had initially attracted me to him was stronger than ever. He had a natural charm, and still does. Everyone loves him for it. Certainly, he swept me off my feet. He was alone that evening and I wondered why, but I accepted his invitation to dine together and he would happily pick up the tab for all three of us… I thought it was quite gallant of him to offer actually. Paul was a kind of prince though, very unlike the men that I had dated before, and unlike Joe who was a quiet man. Paul was much more conscious of making people feel welcome. I loved that about him from the start. He had a social gift as well as a great talent for many things, as I would soon find out. In this, he and I had much in common. We were like two artistic forces coming together and we knew it. In any event, the evening was a delightful reacquaintance and had no feeling of discomfort, the discomfort that might have loomed after our truncated love affair. It was just lovely, but not without a little bit of embarrassment in the end when the bill came; actually, a rather hefty amount of embarrassment as it happens. I'll never forget the look of horror that came over Paul's face when he realized that he had forgotten to bring his wallet. I could see him break into a cold sweat as he searched everywhere for it. We all had a good laugh, of course, and in the end, I wound up paying for his meal. I never imagined this sort of thing fit into a pattern of forgetfulness and such, but nonetheless, that evening was the beginning of our destined journey together.

Paul was a sweet and joyful soul. I knew he had to have flaws but don't we all? It was a relationship meant to be and meant to learn from. It was literally "in the cards." He was the Roman prince my psychic had seen in the Tarot that day. I'd known him before and I would know him again. What a trip.

The sky lit up again with Paul and things moved quickly though we tried to slow them down some. He'd evidently broken it off with the other, many months before and actually left the country for a while. I remember thinking he was quite the adventurer. Fresh out of college he'd moved from Middle America, Colorado, to the big city, and now to London on his own and back again. It was impressive. While I was involved with inner journeying, he was literally journeying, and for him, it was about growing up and becoming a man. All this was meaningful to him and I must say I admired that. He's always tried to do the right thing, to be a good man. Maybe it was his Middle American upbringing, something I had never quite seen before. I think Paul always had in mind to be a hero. Maybe he would be one day. All I knew was that he was my hero, and that was good enough for me.

It seemed that we two had gotten together again by the hand of fate, and we were merely playing those early months out till an inevitable wedding. Our every conversation seemed to have some hidden agenda in which we'd examine each other's correctness for the job. Husband and wife – we were most definitely auditioning for the roles, and everything came up clean, except for those few traits we dared not focus on. Naturally they would come up in time, and we'd inevitably face them. That's the hope of every marriage.

Paul was a good man; that was more important than anything, and we were head over heels. What an amazing adventure we were on. I felt more comfortable with Paul than I'd ever felt with anyone, including Joe. I remember feeling that he was more than my lover. He was all relationships in one, a curious feeling, but true – he was lover, he was brother, he was father, and he was son. He was my family and maybe for the first time, I felt a sense of trust in a man. He engendered that in me. Oh, he warned me that he'd make trouble for me one day. It was already quite clear that he was a "messy" sort. Little did I know this too was connected to a larger pattern... And I wanted to overlook things of this sort because after all, what's a little disorganization? There was no turning back anyway. We had a destiny. We'd been together before and if we hadn't gotten it right back then, we'd find a way to work it out now. I really believed that; I trusted him that much.

There was so much that was right and after all the deliberation, we each passed the audition process. He asked me to marry him and I remember my response was, "Of course". We knew this day would come. It was in the air, but it did come just three months after we had started dating this time around, so the proposal almost seemed surreal after such a speedy courtship. But I said yes and just as quickly, we made plans to move in together to his railroad flat on Avenue B. I sublet my studio and moved in with my cats Jamaica and Montana. We became one big happy family along with Paul's cats, Kitty and Junior. What a menagerie, but that seemed perfectly natural for me as well. I could never imagine marrying a man who didn't love cats. The deal was clinched now. All I had to do was figure out a way to clean up his house and transform it into a thing of beauty. I couldn't live without cats, but neither could I fathom living without beauty. I came into the world with that sensibility. Paul would just have to learn to appreciate it, and like the hero that he had presented himself as, he'd figure out a way to work on things. After all, "cleanliness is next to godliness" in my book and though I say it somewhat in jest, I actually think it is close to the truth. Perhaps more accurately, beauty is next to Godliness and a certain degree of order was necessary to manifest beauty...

Anyway, I tore into that apartment. I helped him organize, painted designer colors on those old beat-up walls, and added my woman's touch. And we set out about our lives with plans to marry.

Our marriage began like a storybook. Paul and I were like a mythical prince and princess. All we needed was an orchestra to play the tune. The truth is our wedding had it all. It was quite the production and put together by our enormous community of friends, all of which were fellow artists and performers. We had a Renaissance theme and held it under two tents at the Queen's Botanical Gardens. What gorgeous splendor! Who needed an enchanted forest? Nothing could possibly compare to this. I made my own wedding dress and if that wasn't enough to put together in just three months, I took it upon myself to create Paul's Renaissance shirt and outfits for the entire wedding party of which there were six more people. It was an incredible feat, but turned out beautifully. My father had given us $3,000 which we brilliantly and creatively stretched. Clearly even for the times, this was small change for a wedding... but perhaps it was par for the course. My father and I were never close past our olden days, but none of that really mattered anymore. Paul's place in my life filled whatever emptiness I had come to know, and really my father was sicker and sicker, so I didn't feel I wanted to push anything on him. It was good enough to know that he'd at least be around to give me away. Perhaps had the money been there for more, the wedding would not have been so sweet and down-to-earth. It was amazing.

Our friends made the food, our friends picked the wildflowers for the tables, and our friends performed. I'll never forget Andre Morgan, who sang one of the most beautiful love songs I've ever heard to date. "There May Come a Day"...

As we walked the garden path a friend who went by the name of Dragonfly played the flute. Everything worked out perfectly despite the rains that had been predicted that never came till later that night. The only thing that might have thrown a wrench into the day was the fact that LaGuardia Airport was so very close and planes were taking off and landing throughout the ceremony.

Alan, who ministered the wedding, set the scene magnificently. He simply said that each plane passing was the voice of God sending blessings from above. Well indeed God was very much with us that day. And with family and friends to hold us in their hearts, it couldn't have been a finer wedding. And the reception was just terrific. Since all of our friends were performers, this turned into an arena that caught the attention of all the passers-by. Crowds actually formed to listen to our band and get a glimpse of what was being performed on the dance floor. We could have sold tickets that day. I always look back with fondness. I've been to many weddings. Nothing was as joyous as ours. What a great time. Just about everyone was there. Even Joe showed up. I believe he missed the ceremony, but was there for the reception with a new girlfriend. They'd flown in from LA and I was simply amazed. I heard from a friend, however, that she spotted the two of them fighting with each other. Evidently Joe hadn't told his lady that I had been more than a friend those many years ago. Somehow, she picked up on it that day and why she would ever feel threatened when I was marrying another man simply did not make sense. But you never know what comes into one's head in affairs of the heart. Joe and I had a special bond. We always wished the best for each other. He had come to my wedding to tell me so. It made it all so much more perfect that he was there. And my father, who was so weak by now, managed to walk with me that day and whatever had stood between us through the years just went away. What a great time.

No one could have asked for a better wedding. At the end of the day a limo came to whisk us back to the city, and we spent our wedding night there at a fancy hotel in Central Park. To top it off, we took a horse and buggy ride through the park in the rain. It couldn't have been more romantic. In the morning we flew off to the Islands for the honeymoon. Paul and I were blessed. We had more fun together than anyone should be allowed, and then on top of it all, we had a honeymoon in heaven as far as I'm concerned. These remain some of the best memories of our lives together. It was all out of a dream and had come so quickly when not long before I had only known tragedy. They say we don't remember pain; I'm not sure that that's true. But certainly, love can heal as long as it's alive, and Paul and I were as loving as any couple could ever have been.

We spent ten days between St. Martin and St. Bart's in the days when they were affordable and still pristine. After a catamaran sail over to St. Bart's we knew that we would have to finish the honeymoon there, though we would have to get there some other way as Paul spent his entire boat trip over in the bellows wretching from seasickness. Of course, to me, being on the sea was like being home. I felt terrible for him, but also, I came to understand that he and I had very different natures when it came to things like this. I had grown up on the ocean. How tragic my husband couldn't quite tolerate it. Fortunately, he appreciated its beauty though, at least from a distance.

We adventured over to St. Bart's not knowing where we would stay. We rented a little jeep and spent the day investigating like Lewis and Clark.

Well, after having combed the island, we happened to run into a most compelling property on the ocean. It was a gorgeous estate and certainly could have been someone's private home, but I felt called to find out one way or the other... and when I hear a calling, I do my best to follow. This was no exception. I prayed it was an inn despite its unusual atmosphere... We never saw a "no trespassing" sign though, so we walked right up to the door and knocked... and hoped for the best...

A very beautiful, darkly tanned young woman answered and fortunately was most gracious, and that was a relief. We expressed our curiosity and so she invited us in. And, with her lovely French accent, told us the history of the place and showed us around.

It was owned by an ex-governor of the island and had been turned into a vacation resort that had done well for a while, but was going through a very dry spell, especially in these out-of-season months. This place was utterly magnificent and had a most extraordinary feeling about it, with Caribbean bungalows set on a stony cliff above the sea. We had the impression that they had shut down the place because so few had shown interest, but it was perfect for us and we hoped that she would let us stay. And it was almost preferable to have the place to ourselves. Astoundingly, she said yes and at 85 dollars a night, we got to live in a villa of our own with God's beloved ocean at our feet.

The first night we stayed in one of their small cliff side cottages, but she gave us the whole house from the next night on. I'll never know what we did to deserve it. We had an amazing suite with the most beautiful four-poster bed and French doors that opened to the ocean. We had the main floor to ourselves and the balcony off of it to boot. They gave us complete access to their professional kitchen the likes of which I've only dreamed of since. And speaking of dreams, I always thought that we'd return to that place. As it turns out, however, we would have had to become millionaires to have done so. It became one of the most exclusive and prohibitive boutique resorts in the world once it was sold and remodeled. But it kept its original name that had described it so perfectly: "Eden Rock."

Paul and I really did get to stay in Eden for our honeymoon. Nothing could have compared. I would love to return; I would love to live somewhere like it – by the ocean, but for now thank heavens for our memory of that most wonderful time. It was only ten days, but they'll go down as ten of the very best days that I've ever known. Sadly, we had to say goodbye and return to our scruffy little abode on Avenue B, New York.

MARRIED LIFE

"Love does not consist of gazing at each other,
but in looking outward together in the same direction."
Antoine de Saint-Exupery

My early days with Paul were perfect. I never wanted for more despite the fact that we lived in a rather sketchy neighborhood and had little money. We made enough. We were creative and between the two of us, we turned that flat into a home studio for many an artistic venture. This was our life, our partnership. And it was held together with harmony and purpose.

I always thought that we would do great things together but it began there in that beat-up old flat. One day we would leave; for now, it was perfection. I never felt unsafe there despite the fact that it was a lower income part of town, and looked it. I suspect we were well taken care of by the locals because Paul had taken care of the neighborhood children. Among his new Vaudevillian skills, he did some clowning for all the Puerto Rican children. They called him Piaso, which meant Clown in Spanish... Paul was definitely the Pied Piper of Avenue B and it's quite possible that because these children loved him so, we were looked after and protected in a neighborhood that could have been a little scary.

Life was good. We were entering a new world together. And it was unlike anything I'd ever known before. It seemed a miracle to me that I, who had lived a solo life, and a good one despite my childhood abandonment issues, was now a married lady ready to settle down. It was hardly fathomable that I would ever be able to build new roots with another human being when I didn't exactly know what it was like to have roots. They had been severed so long ago. But now it seemed, and forevermore, my experience of life would be so very different than what came before... while holding the hand of another... And there was so much ahead that was joyous much of the time, but tragic as well.

The strangest thing of all was now that I had found Paul and was entering my future life with him, all semblance of my past was starting to fade away. My father, who had managed to walk with me on my wedding day, was now dying. I remember going out to visit him in those last months feeling that he was just a ghost of the man that I had known all those years ago. He was thin and frail and left with no fight at all. This was a man with more charisma than almost anyone I'd ever known with the exception of my own husband. Now it was gone and all that was left was suffering. It just killed me to see him this way, and it was clear that he had no way out of his cancer that oddly had gone to his brain, like my mother years before. It was such a peculiar feeling for me to witness his death at this juncture in my life. I felt stretched between the joy of marriage and an awful sadness of losing my father. And his suffering was hard to bear. And worse, I knew he and I would never get a chance to reconcile our relationship. But I'd have to reconcile my many complex feelings in time to come. For now, I could only pray that he wouldn't suffer for long.

Finally, he went into the hospital one last time. One assumes that things will improve somehow. At one's lowest, the docs who we think of as saviors will find a way to make it all right, or at least make one's passing somewhat easier. Sometimes they do. I'm not sure it was the case for my father. It seemed every drug they gave him backfired in some way, and most of them made him crazy or downright delirious. I came to visit him every day and every day I'd hear his tortured scream as I'd get off the elevator. Eventually I just prayed for his passing. I remember wondering what he was holding onto. He'd cry to me and the others to let him go, to just let him go, as if we had the power. Yet it seemed he himself couldn't let go. I wonder to this day how anyone can withstand that sort of endless suffering. But we see it all the time. Is it the terror of death that makes people hold on, or is it the love of life? Eventually God, I suppose, makes us ready. The body and the mind have to suffer to surrender, and it becomes too much to bear. I wonder however, if native cultures, like the old Alaskan tribes, have a far more humane approach when they take their old dying parents to the frozen tundra to be taken by the wilds of the natural world.

When my father finally went into a coma, I would sit with him for hours on a deathwatch. It was the same with my grandfather. I would sometimes speak aloud to him and eventually I told him of my sorrow for our sad, sad relationship, and how I loved him and knew he loved me.

After I'd had my say, I begged him to let go. "Let go Daddy," I said, "It'll be all right. You'll be released." I told him to let go, that it was okay, that it was his time. I didn't know if he heard me, but I hoped that I had some healing effect on him. After all these years of disharmony, I wanted ultimately to help him, and there in that hospital all was forgiven. I only wanted for him to be at peace.

I went home that night in a complete fog. I remember what it was like to be on the Long Island railroad heading back to New York with the feeling of my father's impending death. It all felt unreal somehow. They had just enforced a nonsmoking rule on the train, but being so utterly out of sorts I found myself lighting up cigarette after cigarette without thinking. I didn't know what I was doing. After the third cigarette they threatened to throw me off the train. I remember wanting to cry. I would have cried on the conductor's shoulder for the human dilemma that we all face but rarely talk about – death – but of course, no one cared. We who travel together on trains like this are all strangers to each other. There is little contact and no one knows what's going on inside someone else's soul. I tell you, as I looked around, life seemed insane to me, just insane. A dark shadow had fallen and all I could think was to get back home to Paul as quickly as I could. That old feeling of running like the wind had returned, but this time I had someone to run to, thank God. Thank God I had my husband, and when I got back, he greeted me with open arms.

I'll never forget that night. I think I was somewhere in the ethers when the phone call came in. They told me that Clyde had died. I still wonder if he heard me that night, if I helped him in some way, if I eased his pain. Who knows? I only remember how strange it was to fathom that he was no longer with us, such a vibrant man, such a force with so much to say. Now it was just quiet somehow.

I had been holding so many complex feelings inside me that nothing but love could have tended my heart. And thank God my husband helped me through it. Just three months after we married, Clyde died. We went to his funeral and as I recall, my concerns were more for my sister than for myself. Maybe it was the spiritual work that had helped me, maybe Paul. But these days I look back to my losses and traumas, and I realize that the inner child is forever eternal... That magical spirit is always seeking to live and even flourish despite all else. Maybe it's the inner child that gets us through the death of others.

Maybe it is she that holds our hand in darkness with a tender reminder of the blessings of life. Perhaps she is the one who holds the key to hope and faith, and to renewal.

Years later when I got into the Tarot, the meaning of the archetypes naturally fascinated me, being an artist and a Jungian. But the image of the Fool and his eternal youth is perhaps one I pay most attention to when feeling lowest or in a quagmire. Don't we all feel in a quagmire sometimes, particularly these days? The Fool is like that inner child, so full of spirit and innocence. And it is the Fool who blindly goes forth on his journey taking leaps of faith in the face of danger and sorrow. He is the one who is able to find a creative way to survive despite the worst of circumstances... And it is he, that on some level, whether it's conscious or not, knows that life itself is one big schoolroom and that we are here to learn and hopefully transform. Death of course is the biggest lesson of all. It's the final frontier... But I think universally speaking, when a loved one dies, it brings us to an edge. It's as if we ourselves go forth just far enough to get a glimpse of the eternal. It's a soulful experience for us all and may teach us better how to live, once we've allowed ourselves the right to mourn...

Anyway, we had the funeral and memorial service. I'd certainly been to a few by now and I can say this, some services are actually beautiful. They can be remarkably moving when spirit is brought into the room. I can't say that was the case here. I don't remember much about it but whether I got along with my father or not, it did not seem right to me that a man like Clyde, who for better or for worse, lived like such a force of energy on this planet, would receive such a dull, flat sendoff. His eulogy was no more than a list of facts that read like he had never even lived as far as I was concerned. I don't know. Maybe his faults were too well-known and maybe these people didn't have much to say when all was said and done. But I who even knew how tough a guy he was, wanted more for him than that. Even I knew he did his best.

There was an open casket which was really very eerie. I remember having seen my grandmother Edie shown in this way. It's a bizarre tradition. I gather it's supposed to offer an opportunity to say goodbye. But the soul has flown away by now, and the only thing the sight of an embalmed body does is clinch that message if you didn't grasp it before. It's shocking and it's disturbing. Perhaps it's another one of life's brutal lessons, but I would rather have been left with the image of my father's spirit than the haunting memory of his empty body lying there like that.

I didn't get to my mother's funeral and was never able to say goodbye to her as a result, yet my father's service was no less disheartening. I think because of these two experiences in some way, I was left with an uncanny desire to help usher spirit in and out whenever possible. This feeling grew and grew over the years as an artist and a performer. It remains my utmost goal. But in many ways, I think I had another calling and perhaps it was to be a minister myself... or something like that. I have had many dreams that told me of this mission other than the arts. These dreams always had to do with helping people live spiritually viable lives, and then easing their passing with faith and inspiration, and a soulful offering at the time of service and ceremony. My father seemed to have little of that.

In any event, it was over. We buried him and went on with our lives. We mourned in our own way, but as I said before, the freshness of marriage buffered what might have taken place. Above and beyond all else, I was about to receive the greatest blessing of my life with the miracle of new life growing within... I found out that I was pregnant and I kid you not, the simple math indicated that my child may have been conceived the very night my father died. Paul and I always imagined that those two souls passed each other in the night, but we always wondered what they had said. In any case, once again the sun rose and joy replaced my sorrow.

The coming months were divine. I took to pregnancy like Gaia herself. While other women complained of constant nausea and fatigue, I felt healthier than ever through most of those nine months. The timing of it all was so perfect. The Great Creator must have been on my side because my doctor wasn't certain that I'd ever be able to get pregnant in the first place. I'd had a history of endometriosis, and problems with my ovaries which had indicated it would be a miracle if it was to happen.

I sometimes wonder about the spiritual aspects of conception and birth. They say we all of us choose our parents. I tend to think there's some collusion between souls, particularly when the odds are against it, or at least are challenging. I remember the vision that I'd had in meditation of my floating boy and how I'd felt so strongly that I'd come to this lifetime for him. Was it the same for Shane? I like to think so. I know these many years later there is a psychic bond between us like no other. And we've shared things most sons and mothers don't, though they say the silver cord remains intact far longer in that natural relationship than with daughters. Well, I don't know about the norm; I only know of infinite love when it came to my own mother. Anyway, it was a blessing from God when this little boy came down from the heavens in the face of many odds and physical challenges... I married the man of my dreams and now in time I would hold in my arms the child that I had come to this lifetime to know and to love. What on earth could ever disturb that perfection? "What on earth" was right. And how could it have been seen in the stars?

There are many ways of perceiving life as the tale of Rashomon suggests. When one is hit with extraordinary circumstances, your mythic experience can take you into an underworld of sorts. I suppose having gone through my already dramatic history, the underworld was not unfamiliar to me, but it was unfamiliar to Paul. No one was prepared, however, for what would come up from the simple nip of a Lyme tick. Illness changes the course of one's life. Lyme Disease changed mine, it hurt my son, and I guess it hurt my marriage too.

It happened slowly and then it escalated, and I am still picking up the pieces. Luckily for me, my curiosity of life's mysteries stood tall against the fates. I just feel sad that my boy had to be at the effect of being in utero when I was bitten. Que sera sera... I can still hear my mother's voice. What will be will be. The only blessing of such illness is that the challenge demands that you go even deeper, and you are given the opportunity to sharpen your skill at alchemy.

Anyway, the sun may have eclipsed through illness, but my son, Shane-Luke, despite it all, was pure light. In fact, I remember when I chose the second part of his name, Luke, it seemed perfect to me because it meant "the bringer of light." Oh was he ever, and he remains to be so. It was a wonderful pregnancy. I glowed with the 65 pounds I gained. I needed that extra weight anyway, but we always joked that I looked like I was carrying a torpedo. It was only a few months after we married and Daddy had just died, but I was 35 by now and Paul felt the same about children just as I did – we couldn't have been happier and Paul couldn't have been prouder.

The early testing called CVS informed us at nine weeks that we were having a boy and that he was certainly healthy, thank God. And I went about doing everything I could to keep it that way. I quit smoking immediately. I went on a proper pregnancy diet and read every book on the subject ever printed. I became an expert like mother Nature herself. We ran the gamut of names and finally came up with Shane-Luke, though he goes by the name Shane and often Shaner.

I built a small nursery in the middle of our railroad flat. I may have been pregnant, but I was as determined as ever to create a beautiful home. And since the baby was coming to Avenue B, I was compelled to turn that crazy apartment into a proper home for a child.

Summer was approaching and I remember the climb up to our third-floor apartment was becoming a struggle, and the heat got worse and worse. I waddled around the city, but was relieved any time I could get on the train and head out to the ocean, or to Croton on the Hudson in Westchester for visits with my sister. Periodically I did just that. Stefi and I had grown close over the years, especially now that Clyde had died. We had each other and despite the conflicts that we had growing up with different parents, we were each other's family and that was a blessing. She had her little boy Trevor, and it was exciting to think that there would be cousins between us. Many little miracles...

Anyway, we'd often get together in those days and go down to the Hudson River or any of those magnificent parks in her area. Stefi and Don lived in paradise as far as I was concerned. I love that part of New York State. Actually, I love the whole of New York State. I love the East Coast. And though Manhattan had given me my independence and offered the best of almost everything, fortunately the ocean was just a train ride away. The thick, fertile trees, the rivers, and hills were all a 30-minute ride from the city, and that made me happier than I can ever say.

This summer, I decided as well to take a trip out to Fire Island, a place in all my years in New York I had never been to, but had heard wonderful things about. I can't quite remember why I had gone out there ahead of Paul, but in two nights he was to join me. That was fine. I went out by myself and loved the adventure, particularly the ferry ride over. Once there, I followed the crowds, waddling to my little hotel room. It was a great little vacation away from Manhattan and when Paul arrived, we'd spend each day at the beach. I would have stayed forever, as it felt so natural to be there. I imagined my baby within felt at home as well. I tend to think that on some level, once spirit comes in, beings have some sort of awareness of the environment outside the womb. If so, he'd have enjoyed the rush of waves, the sound of the birds above, and the children's laughter by the shore.

To this day he loves the ocean as I do. Was it in the blood or did it start there in utero? I have to wonder about his innate sense of music, which became evident from infancy. At four months that little baby knew how to match my pitch on cue. He might have been late crawling and sitting, but he was already singing as an infant. Did it have anything to do with the music box that I serenaded him with every night of my pregnancy? I'd set it on my belly and I could just imagine him listening to its tune, "La Vie en Rose." Shane, who became a natural songwriter, admits that as far back as he can remember, he was making music in his head.

In his very early years, we had a dish swing in our backyard. Shane would swing on it for hours. I actually worried a bit about this incessant swinging and wondered what was going on in his little head. Years later he informed me that he'd always been listening to the music from within himself while swinging. Anyway, I always reflect back to the music box, and I reflect back to the ocean that seems to call us.

In any event, it was time to return to the city. I'd miss Fire Island, but we'd return to it as a family someday, or so I thought. For now, a long weekend was good enough and besides, in my last trimester I was starting to have trouble getting around despite the fact that I continued to work at the Mime Theatre, believe it or not. And I had built outrageous costumes that accommodated a pregnant lady like me.

During most of my pregnancy I felt healthier than ever until my seventh month. Almost immediately after my return from Fire Island I broke out into a vicious rash that turned my final months into a nightmare. There was no getting rid of it and I couldn't fathom what prompted it. My obstetrician had never seen anything like it and none of the books that I had read wrote of such a thing. It was truly obscene. And I prayed that the baby wasn't going to be affected. What on earth could it have been, and why couldn't my body shake it off?

Finally, I was sent to a dermatologist who promptly gave me a blood test to rule out an illness that I personally had never heard of, but was apparently becoming an epidemic. He gave me a topical ointment, but as I suspected, it had no effect. Honestly, I couldn't wait to have the baby. It was really too much at this point to carry him like this. And I imagined that he himself wanted out early. How can a living soul, especially in the womb, not feel a mother's stress when it's to such an extreme? This had gone on now for far too long.

I went into labor in early August, 10 days before my due date, when the moon was at its fullest... It may have seemed amusing to others, but all I could think of was thank God. Little did I know it would take another 24 hours and it would be no easy deal. Women love to tell their labor stories; I'm no exception. It's one badge of merit that we get to wear, each one of us, and sometimes the harder the birth the prouder we are! It's unfathomable to me to consider however, that in times past the husband wasn't even present. The woman was usually put into a twilight state and neither parent had any awareness of the birth. Amazing! Pain or no pain, I loved every minute of bringing this baby into the world.

My experience was so powerful that the last thing I was thinking about was my rash. The difficulty of my labor was a great distraction. Like magic, the terrible itching subsided. I was certainly in a primal state of mind, body and soul! And it helped...

There were a few things out of the norm from the get-go, however, aside from my terrible condition with the rash. When I was finally seen in the hospital, they told me that the baby had turned and that I was having something called back labor. That would account for the kind of pain that I was having. Nonetheless I was nowhere dilated enough to be tended to at the hospital so they sent me home... I think in reality, there were no rooms available. Many ladies were giving birth that day because the moon had pushed them to it. I'd have to wait my turn.

And so, after a lot of moaning and groaning on my part, Paul practically carried me out of that hospital and we went back down to Avenue B by taxi. I was not looking forward to climbing those stairs in this condition. Oddly enough, it looked like I might not have to because when we arrived at the building, Paul realized that he didn't have his keys. Who knew where they were? As I mentioned before, we mothers love to tell our tales. Most, however, don't quite get as comical as ours. Life with Paul would often prove to be so. Why not? Everyone knew him as Paiaso.

It was August in Manhattan and it couldn't have been hotter, dirtier, and more humid. I sat down on the sidewalk with my little traveling case and leaned against the building as my hero climbed up the fire escape and broke into our apartment. One thing about Paul that to this day holds true – he can get himself into trouble, but always seems to know just how to remedy almost any fix. He's resourceful; I'll hand him that; and when all else seems to fail, I swear that man has a guardian angel always looking out for him. In any event, he rescued me and I spent the rest of the day waiting for Shane in our third-floor flat. Who knows what happened to the keys?

We invited a friend who studied some midwifery and was a massage therapist. She was a blessing for my interminable labor. Eventually we wound up back at Lennox Hill and this time I would not be sent home. We were assigned a room with another woman in labor, but while others were knocking their babies out, mine was taking his sweet time. And then came the drugs... Now, I was no stranger to drugs and certainly wasn't holding out for a completely natural birth. Oh no, on the contrary, I'd had quite a respect for meds from the beginning. My history going back to childhood had taught me the great merit of Western medicine, and through all my young fevers and deliriums, I'd grown up on it all. I practically lived on antibiotics back then. And then in later years I got through every awful menstrual cycle that had been heightened by endometriosis with painkillers, the best of which was Percodan. Even my flirtation with recreational drugs in Woodstock proved to be, oh I don't know, beneficial in some bizarre way. I tried many of them and never had a problem.

I was fully prepared to take drugs if they were offered and I never expected to have adverse reactions, but indeed I did. They prepared something that was referred to as the "cocktail drip." I'd heard about this and after hours of back labor, I was all for it. I was told that I would get a nice, steady flow of Demerol to take the edge off, and that sounded just fine to me. But I simply could not handle it. I suspect this was the precursor to the profound chemical sensitivities I'd come to know in time...

In any event, this "cocktail" had triggered a bit of an emergency and so they removed the drip as fast as they could... My sensitivity to it was obviously peculiar, but I never understood why anyone would opt to be the least bit non-present for the arrival of their baby anyway. Had I known that this was to be the case, I would never have agreed to it. However, between the back labor, the reaction to meds, and the number of hours I'd been working at it, they were considering me high risk at this point. I remember being given Pitocin to hurry the process along with an epidural... There seemed to me to be an awful lot of hoopla, with a number of docs and nurses hovering. I assumed something had gone a bit awry. But the worst was to come when a young intern burst into the room in a panic. He had some lab results that had just come in and they were not good... "Erica Sarzin-Borrillo? Are you the one who recently was tested for Lyme disease?" Good Lord! Everyone turned around in shock! On the heels of announcing the results, which were obviously positive, the docs shooed him away as fast as possible... What a way to learn such news... Lyme Disease. I remember panicking. I think the whole room fell into an emergency state and I was rushed on oxygen but it took a while to settle me down. I loved the primal nature of giving birth, but regret that moment in time when I learned I had Lyme Disease. Then again, I never knew what would come of it, because if I had, I might have done things differently. Who knows? The question of destiny always comes into play when it comes to such things.

In any event, I did calm down enough to not only live through the news, but get through the rest of the labor and finally get enough feeling back into my body to do what I needed, to birth my baby. Up until now I was a so-called good patient, a patient who did whatever the docs had suggested. After 24 hours my wild woman instincts kicked in... I remember telling my husband I was going to have to get primal. I think he knew I meant business and in retrospect, he and I were indeed proud of how we proceeded. When everyone finally left us all alone, Paul helped me crawl to the edge of the hospital bed and get on my haunches and start pushing... like an animal... Nothing would stop me now. What power I summoned – amazing. And lo and behold, my baby started to crown. The nurses freaked out when they entered the room. There was complete hysteria and it was hysterical to us. Even my doctor panicked. My God, how far civilization has come from its natural roots. All I know is that I might have laid there for 36 hours instead of 24 had I not trusted gravity and my own phenomenal power.

They rushed me down the hall to the delivery room, while I howled like a banshee all the way. I may have seemed delirious but I'll never forget any of it, and to this day I'm grateful that my husband and I shared the experience. As Shane came into the world, I remember the doctor saying that he was "sunny-side-up". He said one percent of babies are born that way. And, as well, the doctor said in all his years as an obstetrician, he'd never seen a more focused baby. It's fascinating in retrospect as Shane came to grapple with focus issues down the road. I guess his little genius was apparent on the day of his birth, however, as he came out screaming... He had a loud, clear voice that could outmatch my primal scream any day, and a tight little grip too, because when they tried to hand him over to Paul, he clung to the nurse's lapel and his fingers had to be pried off.

Finally, my baby was born and with all fingers and toes, and no rash like mine – that was our biggest fear. What did we know of Lyme Disease? We really only thought in terms of the rash. Since he was clear of that, we just lay back and celebrated Shane-Luke's arrival. I was exhausted, though Paul looked more so. He looked ravaged. We rarely think of what the husband goes through at such a time, but it's a huge event for them. Shane was born at 10:30 p.m. August 3rd around the full moon, and life would never be the same. He was our only child as the Lyme Disease had altered my system so much that after a blighted ovum four months later, I guess I'd become infertile. I would have liked to have had another, a girl, a little sister to Shane, but it was evidently not meant to be. And perhaps it would have been too much for me after the sickness eventually kicked in. Perhaps it was right for Shane to be our only one as well, because he'd been compromised by that peculiar illness himself.

In the early days, our family bonding overshadowed our concerns about Lyme Disease anyway, and we all just fell in love with each other. We brought our little boy back to Avenue B and we went forward with our lives. I never took the course of antibiotics that routinely is prescribed because I was a new mother and wanted to protect my child from the ill effects of Tetracycline... Besides, no one wanted to believe how serious an issue Lyme could be. My rash disappeared within a few days after birth, so Paul and I dismissed it. And the doctors did too.

I nursed Shane for a while. The funny thing is I could have gone on antibiotics and I should have, because we had to put Shane on the bottle almost immediately anyway. He had developed a vicious case of thrush and nursing aggravated it horribly. No baby cried like mine;

it was incredible. Meds did nothing to relieve his pain and finally through the advice of an herbal shop, I swabbed his little mouth with something called gentian violet. It did the trick, though he had purple-stained lips for weeks. There were a few signs that indicated there might be trouble, but we met each challenge one step at a time.

Early on, Shane had seizures in his sleep. Oddly, his pediatrician didn't seem concerned. I always wondered why, and back then I had no reason to distrust the medical profession. The doctor did remark, however, on the baby's rather wild growth rate within his first three weeks. Shane had been born a very normal height and weight, though his footprint went off the charts like the paw of a big puppy. The doctor said it's the rate of growth that often predicts what will come to be in terms of height. At three weeks of age Shane was predicted to reach 6'8". Oh my God! I can't tell you what it's like to hold your delicate baby knowing he'll grow to be that tall one day. But the doctor was absolutely right and Shane always towered over everyone. I remember carrying him in my arms while he'd dangle down to my knees. He looked like a baby giant, but one who was also delicate, and thin. I remember a friend remarked when Shane was still an infant that he looked a little unearthly. Well… I always felt that I had come from a long line of eccentrics. What could one do? He'd know too what it would feel like to be somewhat unusual.

Often what comes with the territory of being tall in stature, and thin as well, is a sensitive nature. That was undeniably true. He's an amazingly gentle young man to this day and he was always the sweetest child, though a whirling dervish for years – a kid with phenomenal energy, particularly after his bout with a fever of unknown origin. It would have been hard to imagine that he'd wind up such a pistol after such young health issues that put him in the hospital at nine weeks with a spinal tap to boot. A mother never forgets her infant's scream. It was horrifying. He was on IV for over a week and they never did find out what it was. I always wondered if it was some elusive manifestation of being in utero when I contracted Lyme. I still wonder… Who knows?

I'd had a terrible stomach flu, or so I thought, earlier that week. I remember thinking the cramping was worse than labor, but I did get through it. Was it all early Lyme? Anyone who has suffered from Lyme Disease knows that it's an impossible disease to deal with, and controversial. It's called "the great imposter" because it can imitate any and all diseases. The spirochete inevitably mutates so that blood tests can't be counted on and many lose their tolerance for drugs and herbs, so treatment gets to be very tricky. Well, that happened to me. Worst of all, insurance companies want no part of it because this illness has an endless, cascading health profile that is cost-prohibitive. It's pitiful quite frankly, and no one has compassion or understanding. But that's another story (but the story of my life).

At the time, when Shane and I were first having health issues, I never thought to attribute it to Lyme. We got through everything just fine, and we moved on with our lives, and we simply thought that we would live happily ever after. No reason to think otherwise. In any event, once our initial ailments disappeared, Lyme Disease was the last thing to take my focus. Whether it was a reality or not, ignorance was bliss, and so was being a mother.

We spent the next ten months together on Avenue B... Shane-Luke was born in New York and a born New Yorker like his mother and his father, who moved to Colorado when he was two and a half. We would leave with Shane when he was 10 months old. We'd enjoyed our early days in the city but knew that we would be hard-pressed to actually raise him there, especially on the Lower East Side. I'd have opted to be near the ocean or the Hudson River like my sister, but the money wasn't there. I've always regretted that, but at the same time Paul's parents were alive, mine were not, and we wanted Shane to be around grandparents. I suppose there was some musing in the beginning about the possibility of leaving, but really having him with us in New York was wonderful. I brought him to mother/baby groups, to friends, all of whom adopted him as their own, and to Croton. I had no parents, but I had my sister, my stepbrother, my cousins and aunts and uncles and, I must say, there's nothing like a baby to bring family members together.

But life can change quickly and our journey certainly took a different course on the turn of a dime. Oh, it's possible that the decision to leave NY was a bit impulsive, but I remember telling Paul that if Colorado didn't work out for any reason, we could always move back. At the time the move seemed the only viable thing to do and I was the one who instigated it, interestingly enough.

Here's the pivotal story: I had been out one day with Shane strolling down Union Square. It was not unusual; I was always out and about with him, and the day was simply gorgeous. But something happened out of the blue that resulted in my turning on my heels and racing back home with an announcement that it was time to get the hell out of Manhattan. I explained to Paul what had happened. It seemed to be the clincher to a long enough line of negative New York stories, though I only remember this one.

Shane and I had been enjoying our little stroll when all of a sudden, a derelict appeared and started heading towards us in an aggressive manner, to say the least... He was weaving in a stupor with so much steam that I knew I would have to act quickly. mothers have protective instincts, or perhaps you could call them archaic remnants the likes of which are truly primal. And I'll say this; when they rise up, even a skinny lady like me will transform. Like a wolf, I threw myself in front of the baby carriage and summoned an ear shattering howl from within my wilds. I scared the daylights out of that drunken bum and he ran off with his tail between his legs. Everyone on the street was simply stunned. But that was it – I wanted out.

We left within the month. We sold our lease, I handed my Gramercy sublet over to my renter, and we said our goodbyes to everyone. And like that we all went forward like pioneers. We took a fork in the road I never expected that led us down a very different path... And that path had some great opportunities, but some very difficult obstacles as well. I am reminded of an astrological reading that pinpointed the so-called "eclipse of my life's light" that was to take place right here in 1989.

Oh God, I'd come so far from my childhood traumas, and truly found great happiness with my husband and beautiful boy. What could possibly darken my world? What indeed. I don't mean to say that life was so black-and-white as all that. I do mean to say, however, that the conflicts that came to emerge were not easily dismissed or gotten through. They were more of an impossible situation that I would struggle with for years to come. Thank God life itself seeks balance even on the most abstract level, and certainly it is when one finds oneself in an impossible situation that actual growth can take place. I'm reminded now of a quote by Carl Jung I've always been drawn to that refers to this.

"The unconscious always tries to produce an impossible situation in order to force the individual to bring out his very best. Otherwise, one stops short of one's best, or does not realize oneself. What is needed is

an impossible situation where one has to renounce one's own will and
one's own wit and do nothing but wait and trust to the impersonal
power of growth and development." C.G. Jung from Spring, 1962.

Well indeed. The next 18 years of my life did present such a situation. And if I look beyond whatever I may have suffered, I have to admit it was now that I was brought to my deepest exploration of life's mysteries. Oh yes, once initiated into serious illness, there is no denying the spiritual lessons that come up… or that you are brought "down to". The devastating effects of Lyme were evidently unleashed by the move. And through my experience with this illness, I found myself facing philosophical questions of all time. There was no doubt that some rather profound spiritual journeying was taking place in any event.

Some understand what it means to live with an impossible illness. And when I say impossible, I refer to the kind that is untenable, because not only is it incurable, but there is no course of action to take to lift one's suffering. Illness of this sort feels mythic. I actually became well acquainted with the myths of Inanna and Persephone that dealt with the underworld… with descent and the stripping away layer after layer of armor, ego, and adornment. Believe me, such illness will lay you bare only to question everything… including your very purpose and more importantly, God.

Profound illness is what I met in Colorado within the first month of my move. Interestingly enough I had found out that it may very well be the move from sea level to such an altitude that triggers a number of autoimmune disorders, MS being one, Lupus another, and Lyme, once the poisonous spirochete has forever altered the system. I never imagined though, how badly I would suffer and how it would kick in my lifelong issues of abandonment and once again freedom. Now I would feel more and more like the bird on the wire who tries in its own way to be free.

We had moved into the basement of Paul's parents' home. Tony and Dot were most gracious and naturally so happy to have their son back, and now their first grandchild. I felt displaced, however, and a bit like a vagabond. But I knew we would eventually have our own home. It was an exciting adventure, though mixed for me now that the actual move had taken place. I suppose I was a little in shock for many reasons actually. Perhaps I was starting to get sick. Who knows? But I recall my early impressions despite the fact that I dismissed my feelings in the moment. They came up over and over again. What could I do? I felt like a stranger in a strange land.

I remember taking Shane for walks that summer and feeling a sinking sense of loneliness and not because I had no friends. No, no. It never occurred to me that I would ever have trouble making friends; I never had trouble before. But truly I couldn't help but feel the uncanny difference in the energy and the atmosphere. This was no doubt the culture shock of having lived in the most alive and stimulating of towns to what seemed here to be the opposite. But it wasn't that alone... It was the lack of hill and dale, of fertile land that I'd known thick with trees, the sea, and the air, no matter how far from the shoreline I was. Oh God, I knew it from the beginning and as much as I tried to put it out of my mind, I knew I didn't quite belong here on a soul level. But New York City was no longer an option once our little one came into our lives. This was to become another aspect of my "impossible situation", because honestly in the end, I truly believe every soul has a home and a natural environment where he thrives.

I remember a dream of mine that I'd had some years ago that revealed what I always felt was, in fact, my soul's home. I always fancied that dream had something to do with my inner archetype, the High Priestess. Let me describe it to you.

> I was in an ancient and foreign land, though not foreign to me. It felt like my secret home. I was in a boat floating through a magnificent waterway and through majestic willows weeping and throwing their gorgeous leaves. This environment was so peaceful and utterly soothing to my soul. Though I was the only one here, I did not feel lonely. I felt at one with everything and entirely harmonious. On the final bend of the river I saw through the leaves of a great weeping willow an amazing display of mosaics. A whole variety of colors and structures revealed themselves as I approached the shoreline. And before me stood a glorious mosaic temple. I got off the boat and disappeared into this great place of meditation, and I know that it belonged to me and was my home for eons. I still see the great temple in my mind's eye and visualize myself dressed as the High Priestess, meditating somewhere within its walls.

It's many years later and honestly; my soul still longs for its home. Some would say it's not just a dream but dreaminess. But somewhere inside I know where I belong. But now, though I live in Denver in my husband's homeland, I have designed our house to reflect that most calming atmosphere, with greens all over and the feeling of some ancient spiritual land. Some have said it looks Balinese and, as it happens, I believe for many reasons that I actually had a lifetime there. To this day I dream of going home to the ocean, but rarely mention it to my husband who evidently had a different dream. And through these years, our many differences would be thrown into the mix of my "impossible situation," as Carl Jung had so aptly put.

Through it all however, there were more blessings than I could ever begin to tell by way of my continued creative life, both through the entertainment business we had developed, and artistically as a writer, painter and actress. Of course, I am ever so grateful to have known the Borrillo clan and to have come to love them, particularly Paul's father, Tony, who genuinely made me feel a part of that clan. But in the end, I'll have to say the blessing of all time has been in bringing up my beautiful boy, Shane-Luke, my little "bringer of light". There's a beautiful saying by Joseph Campbell: "The goal of your life is to match the heartbeat of the universe". Children can remind you of such things; Shane did. He brought the light to me, though my own may very well have been eclipsed, and he brought to me one of the most beautiful heartbeats I'd ever heard.

We lived in Wheat Ridge, Colorado with Paul's parents for a couple of months in 1989. Shane had his first birthday there and took his very first steps on that celebrated day. How could he have shown such talent with such fine timing? I always found each stage of infancy through toddlerhood an absolute miracle. I'll never forget when he was only a couple of months old. He learned to put his little hands together for the first time and I thought the earth stood still in that moment. Oh, how I applauded him! I could see how he knew in that very moment, the glory of a good performance. Only months old, maybe even weeks, and already he knew about the limelight. I have to admit, for better or for worse, it might have been my fault, but this little boy was already conscious of himself and the possibility of moving another human being in his world.

To me, this is a most fascinating aspect of the human psyche. Self-consciousness is a trait that belongs to the Human alone. I suspect therein lies our greatest gift and our greatest curse. It's the stuff that makes us reach for the stars I suppose, but it's also the stuff that makes the human animal ultimately neurotic. Anyway, I had a real live boy and proud parents that we were, we felt utterly blessed to watch his little life unfold. I wondered in the beginning if we ever would bond, however, because he always seemed so distressed by thrush. One could rarely soothe his nervous system, which had obviously been compromised. Of course, the bonding came and still remains. And I am grateful for all my precious memories and for the boy that God gave to me.

And so, Shane turned one on August 3rd and we began to hunt around for our first home. With Tony as cosigner, we knew a starter home would be possible. It would have to be meager, however, on the little income that we would be making. We wouldn't be able to afford a house in the mountains where the magnificence of Colorado existed, revealing the nature of God's country. No. Nor would we be able to afford to live in Boulder, which had truly appealed to me, as it was very beautiful, stimulating and had a leaning toward spiritual activity. I thought it would have suited us, but it wasn't possible.

We were happy to get what was viable at the time and so the papers were signed. We were to move sometime in September. Good. It was time to move out on our own and start our own life, and besides, it was becoming obvious that Paul's parents wanted their lives back as well. How long can one stay without becoming a burden of sorts? And, I have to admit I'm fairly certain it was beginning to feel that way to some extent, particularly because I was now experiencing my first real flare-up of the Lyme Disease. And, as unbearable as it was for me, I felt it was a hardship for everyone around me as well. This was my first realization of how personal illness is perceived by even the most loving people. It doesn't seem fair, but most folks really can't handle it, let alone be truly nurturing or sympathetic for that matter.

THE DARK NIGHT

"This limbo… which lasted timeless days,
started as torment, but turned into patience, started as Hell,
but became a purgatorial dark night, humbled me, took away hope,
but then sweetly, gently, returned it to me thousand-fold, transformed."
Oliver Sacks

I was horribly ill, sicker than I'd ever known possible. It was as if the world was caving in on me, taking me down with crippling fatigue and outrageous pain, that I later learned was Fibromyalgia. I remember falling to the floor in excruciating pain with tears streaming down my face. Paul would cradle me and do his best to offer prayer and even crystal healings, though he had no prior experience with it. It was simply tragic to lay incapacitated like that when Shane obviously needed me. I suppose there were times he thought it was some kind of game, of child's play, but honestly, it mortifies me that Shane had to grow up with a sick mother. He had no choice but to experience it over and over, and each time I would go into some variant of that initial flare-up. Soon we would be leaving Paul's parents. They wouldn't have to be exposed to my illness, but my little family would. How they would come to handle it we would know in time. How I would handle it was my own lonely story, but one never gets used to bouts of devastating illness and being basically shunned for it.

Many years later I ran across a book I cherish to this day called *"The Alchemy of Illness"* by Kat Duff. I recommend it to anyone who is remotely in a situation like mine. It was a great solace for me, perhaps because there was a similarity between us to begin with. She being a Jungian as I was, spoke like a soul mate who finally understood everything that I was going through. Even her illness was of a similar nature. She had Chronic Fatigue Syndrome as well... CFS is a condition that evidently manifests from the cascading effects of several different disease processes... Mine obviously came from Lyme... Most doctors don't know what to do with such conditions. There are a few who claim to be experts, but really offer little help. Victims fall through the cracks. In Europe it's aptly called Myalgic Encephalomyelitis, a much more accurate name. It is thought to be a kind of post-encephalitis. That seems to resonate with me.

I remember that marvelous film, "Awakenings," with Robin Williams and Robert DeNiro. It was based on a case study of Oliver Sack's, about a man who had fallen into a dead sleep after a bout of encephalitis and never woke up till given an experimental concoction of Dopamine. It was a most tragic story because in the end, there was simply no way to control the neurological system and eventually he fell back into a lifelong sleep. CFS is a systemic and neurological condition and one of the many early symptoms of Lyme Disease, along with fibromyalgia.

Through reading everything I could get my hands on, I realized that indeed I was suffering from just that in the early months. Thank God at the time I was still able to take just about anything and so I did. I went about the most vigilant detox program imaginable and built myself up again with herbal concoctions, chiropractic care and acupuncture. And I seemed to kick ill health within a couple of months. Believe me, one bout of the illness was enough for a lifetime, and I never assumed it would return and grow into a monster. But of course, it did! It returned many times over and I must say I am kind of amazed that I have gotten through my evolving flare ups each time. I'm still vulnerable to it though, as it always seems to be lurking about, I suppose, just around the corner. Like a vampire, it can steal your breath away and with it, all semblance of chi, and of heart, and of soul.

No one understood. So, life for me became an intriguing flip-flop back-and-forth between being basically healthy for long chunks of time, which was somehow considered "normal," and being very ill, ill where I would have to hide away for months because one is anything but "normal" when this kind of illness strikes. The truth is one's soul doesn't necessarily reside in the more social world so full of what we consider "normalcy" anyway... No, the soul lives in a deep place and its ultimate resurrection takes moving into it through some form of experience. This is why I fully believe crises of many sorts point to the way of a spiritual healing... And that the wound is indeed the way... I will also say this... every time I was taken down into the world of Hades, I felt a kind of death... and though I completely resonate with John Donne's sentiment, "A sick bed is a grave", I can't honestly say that I consider that a negative. Of course, I wouldn't wish my illness on my worst enemy, but had I not looked at its transformational power, or the potential alchemy of my illness, I wouldn't have been able to live with myself... These days there is a simple phrase: "Find the blessing in everything." Well, that is an amazing lesson and very difficult to achieve, and it's certainly not easy to fathom in the throes of devastation. One has no choice, however, at such times, but to "get real," deathly real, and love what is...

I never bought into the new age assessment about sickly folks... that they're somehow bringing it on themselves. There are judgements made against so many who've been struck down by obstacles of all sorts. But it seems particularly arrogant to judge those with chronic illness. Must we bear not only the suffering, but the stigma of some unholy, dispassionate notion that we ourselves created it along with neediness and victimhood? I believe this perspective holds little understanding of how spirit actually works... or even the understanding that for the sake of one's soul a kind of "descent" sometimes becomes necessary... I've lived with this shaming and so have most with chronic health issues. But then, the rules made by healthy "normal" folk have little meaning in the underworld... and they really know nothing of that mysterious place that illness takes you to. I suppose they can't help but make judgments from the outside looking in... judgments that presuppose sick people are somehow lonely and weak, or in some way have created their own infirmity by being less than perfect. Perhaps they even deserve it... karma.

All this may be unconscious but is rampant and why? Because ultimately one's world is threatened by illness, as if we who know the darkness of disease have fallen from grace. I come in and out of illness and of health, and I have had to learn to navigate well. I have seen the world through both sides and, as a result, I am privy to some things in the human condition that most are not. But illness has also made me far more cognizant of spirit, and if nothing else is said about ill health, it indeed while making one question God, makes one reach to Her more fervently than ever. That is the truth! And I know it through experience.

As you might imagine, illness like mine tends to aggravate one's deepest issues, both psychologically and spiritually. But perhaps we ought to be thanking our bodies for showing us "the way of the wound", because while suspended in the depths, our traumas seem to get dislodged somehow… traumas that were perhaps seemingly packed away. The truth is of course, repression burdens one's soul by the sheer weight of condemning pieces of ourselves to the shadow of our psyches!

I know I've made of my life a living canvas of creativity and yes, my "magical child" carries me well. But perhaps it's been a lot to ask of her. I also know that indeed if "the wound is the way", then healing can never come of avoidance, but of revisits to our original wounds. I do wonder sometimes if my illness, strange as it may seem, might not just be the medicine itself… And one that is Homeopathic by nature!

Naturally I never bargained for such a thing, but I believe like Kat Duff suggests, that there is Alchemy in Illness… And it becomes part of one's journey in the most profound way. For a very, very long time, however, I felt the deepest sense of guilt to expose my little family to my turmoil, because in a way it became theirs. Some husbands actually leave their wives when illness ravages them beyond recognition. Paul never left me, and did his best under the circumstances…

In those days, of course, betwixt and between my flare-ups, my primary focus was Shane. Through the early years I really didn't work and, though one would think bringing up a baby and dealing with an illness was quite enough, eventually my yearning for the creative life that I'd always thrived on would kick in. It would be years before I'd get back to it though, and it's quite possible that its lack in my life left me feeling somewhat out-of-sorts to say the least. Paul was rarely home back then. While carving out his role as the primary caregiver, it gave him the opportunity to develop a life for himself in Denver. In the beginning, of course, he would take anything that would come along to pay the bills and actually, he was a waiter for a while. But soon he was asked to join the Denver Center for the Performing Arts, the regional repertory company.

This was an amazing step for Paul; we were all so proud. But if he hadn't been around much before, his grueling schedule at the theatre made me feel like a single mother.

Looking back on it like this, I begin to understand how Shane and I formed the bond that we did. For me, he was all that I had, and I devoted myself to him, and he seemed equally devoted to me. He was such a little guy but when I'd have my awful flare ups, he would gather my crystals and line them up and down my back, playing the role of healer! I must admit while lying there in my near stupors, I was comforted by his little hands. I suppose we knew how to take care of each other.

I'd been through courses of antibiotics and finally went to an infectious disease doctor who put me on home IV through a Groshong catheter. I was very determined back then about curing the Lyme Disease and was convinced that it was possible to do so. I'd been on the treatment for about three weeks when one night, I had an outrageous toxic reaction of some sort. No one was certain why. It might have been what was known as a Herxheimer reaction. (detoxification reaction with chills, hypotension, flu like symptoms and more) The treatment was stopped and the catheter was re-moved... The doctor put me on antibiotics for months after but eventually I went off meds as chemical sensitivities were setting in... After a while it became clear the doctors couldn't help... and no doubt no longer wanted to deal with my kind of health issues... I really can't say I blame them... But honestly, this illness does get swept under the rug after a while. It's considered the great imposter that carries the vibration of all illnesses and as such can look a little like mental illness! Truth be told many victims of late Lyme literally lose their minds. Well, imagine this, the invading spirochete is actually, in fact, the cousin to syphilis. Symptoms morph and attack the body on many levels and in many ways if you weren't lucky enough to catch it early on. I wasn't one of the lucky ones...

Oh, how I wished for my old life back, for the health that I had once known. But disease was now etched in stone, and it would color everything from now on, whether I liked it or not, whether Paul liked it or not, and he didn't; he couldn't bear it.

And so, Lyme was a true pivotal point in my life. It did present the kind of impossible situation Carl Jung spoke of. Perhaps one day I would come to understand how it grew me but for now, I would need to find a way to tend to my soul in the face of that impossible situation.

3

MY RENAISSANCE

"Artistic process brings Grace.
Does this mean that creativity
is a form of escape or actual presence?
Certainly, we artists enter
a "timeless state of being",
but my experience with creativity
is one of uncanny coherence and flow.
I've come to understand that art
is a collaboration with the divine,
but the venture is not one of transcendence.
It is rather the embodiment of Spirit,
and moreover, when we make Beauty,
we are grounding a piece of Eternity
to behold forever more."
                    Erica Sarzin-Borrillo

It has been 11 full years since I wrote the bulk of these memoirs. I'd spent a good deal of time back then in daily writing rituals, revisiting the dramas, traumas and joys of my life up until the age of 40. And then I simply couldn't go on... I couldn't go on writing about my difficult life because it was time to go on living my life. One might wonder why however, after putting so much into it that I'd leave it for so many years. Well, the fact is, I'm ready now and am here to tell the tale of the past 27 years that followed in a slightly different way.

First of all, on the heels of how my memoirs ended, by this time I think I'm living proof to the idea that "the wound is the way." I can only pray that will come to be the case with the world wounding we all presently face.

I should frame a little of these 27 years gone by, which incidentally are most of my son's life... And most of my marriage. (We will be celebrating 33 years together in August. And Shane will be celebrating his 2-year anniversary with his beautiful wife Christine.)

Life is a but a flash in time, relatively speaking. But of course, so much has happened with much to tell... Tragically, our Mado who lived with us on and off for years is no longer with us... and I must admit I miss her ever so much. You might imagine how it fills my heart to recall her words, "Erica, you are the daughter I never had". She will be remembered always because some relationships are of the soul. Ours was. And then there was another Soul-to-Soul bond that fills me in a similar sense. Our Anna who lived with us for a year and with whom we continue to share a close and loving relationship was for me, "the daughter I never had"... She was our exchange student from the Netherlands who came to us after Shane graduated... She is a beautiful young woman now and a true blessing...

Beyond the stories of which there are plenty more if I put my mind to everyday tales, I would rather say this: Though I continued my life long struggle with Lyme, what seemed to walk hand in hand with my fateful descents, was an explosion of creativity. It was like I lived many a death yet many resurrections.

Through the years, my life was filled with the richness of being a part of Denver's acting community. I was more than grateful to work with Ed Baierlein of Germinal Stage Denver. In NY, I might not have landed certain roles because of my somewhat "exotic type". But Ed respected my ability and willingness to play a variety of characters. With Ed, I got to exercise "the multitudes" within and give them life. And as you might imagine, for one who held such a vested interest in her own soul's growth, living those many characters couldn't have been a more perfect pathway.

Once Shane was old enough for preschool, I started auditioning around town. There were very few union theatres at that time, however. And though I'd been brought in several times to The Denver Center, and was told, "It's just going to be a matter of time, Erica", I was too itchy to get back on the boards. So, I gave up my union card, and started working for Ed. The truth is, I felt blessed to have found Germinal Stage Ensemble. I rather have always liked small arts organizations that engaged in the kind of work he did. I always had trouble with the constant need, inherent in the theatre world that put you in the position of having to prove yourself over and over again. And whether it be in theatre or just about anywhere, when politics or prejudice exists in the market place, the Soul inevitably gets compromised. I will admit, I'm delicate when it comes to that. On the other hand, the soul will find its way. Mine did.

And so, I began a long and fruitful relationship with Germinal and later with other local theatres as well. My experience with each character was a blessing, but of course unlike film making, the stage experience slips away once the show closes. Oh yes, they may remain alive through memory and hopefully through the impact they made on the actor and the audience… But I loved some of those fine author's quotes so much so that I like to think they became a part of me… Some say, if we actors do well enough by the character then we become co-authors while bringing the theatre experience alive.

But the blessing of all time was "Jacques Brel is Alive and Well and Living in Paris", despite the hardships I went through with my first production. I had the great privilege of performing several more and each were career highlights. I can't help feel the many ways Brel had been an extraordinary mentor from early on and remained so through my elder years. His lyrics got inside me and taught me the way of humanity because he himself was an extraordinary Humanist.

As I look back, I feel having "lived" inside the skin of oh so many heroines and such, I can safely say it's been a rich and full 27 years.

But still, the acting experience doesn't fully describe the Renaissance nature of my life... During these years while raising Shane I lived the creative life my first mentor Paul Curtis hoped would be the case for all his students and company members.

I have lived and breathed art of all sorts indeed, and continue to do so despite heart disease or the difficult times we live in. There are many reasons for the way things turn out, the first of which always points to the way of one's Soul of course... with all the various choices that come one's way.

And speaking of "what comes one's way", this brings me to my experience of Julia Cameron's extraordinary book, "The Artist's Way". My word, how it changed my life. Or shall I say, expanded my life. And perhaps, as it clearly has done for thousands worldwide, it gave me so much more freedom than ever before to express myself... and to do so in ways I never dreamed possible.

For those unfamiliar with Cameron's book, it has been used far and wide for years now, bringing artists together wanting to unblock and open to whatever genius laid within.

I found the *"The Artist's Way"* process so profoundly stimulating and successful that I workshopped with several different groups over the years... (around 6... maybe more) Each time it took me to new levels of artistry and spiritual connectivity.

Certainly, if there was ever a Renaissance artist within that wanted out, I'd have to give credit to this very book, and as I think about it, perhaps one workshop in particular. As you can imagine, each group had a different dynamic of its very own. The one I'm referring to now was headed by an unusually talented artist who had much to offer alongside the book's inherent content. In fact, there was something she introduced me to so pivotal that I consider it one of great blessings of my life... It was and still seems to give me a direct line to Spirit... and to the Spirit of the arts. What I'm referring to is something called Visual Journaling. I have stacks of large books I've created, many have called "Holy", that became the artful element of my morning rituals. And as such they kept me "plugged in" to my deeper self and in dialogue with the Divine.

Of course, as Paul Curtis told me years before, I may have fallen from the womb a baby artist, but the Visual Journaling was evidently meant to be the tool I'd need to come fully into my own! Those pages I created every morning turned me into a painter, an author of mystical poetry, a healing artist, and so much more...

In this grand quantum Universe, there is much information we potentially have access to through a variety of ways. And this has been a time of awakenings for so many through many pathways... It is also true that we may need to "change up" those pathways periodically in order to stay stimulated and in a state of awe and playfulness. It just so happens that for me, visual journaling took me to my center every day for years and kept the downloads coming... They opened the channels to conversations with the Beloved, with the Goddess, The Great mother, and the Masters... And thus, an ecstatically-charged spiritual expansion came through me... and grew me through this creative process.

Yes, these were my Renaissance days... Certainly, these were the days I felt the sense of coalescence far more often than not... And interestingly enough that sense of wholeness, though it's the "goal" of one's journey, it never really felt like I'd reached the end-all or "the destination". No, it rather opened me to the idea of higher education in the arena of higher spirit, I suppose. I keep thinking of that expression; "when the soul is ready and willing"... well, I would have to say from my own experience that the phrase would end like this: When the soul is ready, the Universe will indeed conspire to make life work out quite perfectly and as it was intended... Perhaps things fall into place because in truth, life simply mirrors itself... Coalescence within "attracts" coalescence without. It may be the law of the Tao... In any event, I can say it in simpler terms: I was in a state of grace and grace brought me just about everything I needed... Including mentors, I might not have been ready for until this moment in time.

Jean Houston was such a mentor. I consider her to be one of the most brilliant women to ever have graced this planet. Jean held the carrot of knowledge for everything I hungered to learn or learn very much more about. When I met her, I had already built a healing arts practice called "Mythic Healing Arts", and was more than dabbling in many areas that Jean was a virtual genius at. And so, I simply couldn't resist the urge to know this magnificent woman. At age 60 I was re-entering the role of student. Of course, we never truly give that role up, or shouldn't... The Fool within must keep learning, yes? As wise as any of us may ever become, it's the openness of the "beginner's mind" that has the capacity to continually expand... Indeed, the blending of certain energies, or archetypal patterns that take the form of the wise fool may very well hold the key to one's highest potential...

In any event, I did a couple of on-line courses of Jean's, a few weekend retreats and three "salons" in her home. Fascinating... all of them... One important area of study with Jean that strikes me in this moment was the theory of what she calls "polyphrenia", which describes the theory of the inner characters that live within us... Inner characters again. I'd never known anyone outside of Paul who'd envisioned this idea...

Here's Jean on the subject:

"People are essentially polyphrenic. Schizophrenia is a disease of the Human condition, and polyphrenia (the orchestration of our many selves) is our extended health. We have a cast crew within, that used to be called sub-personalities. But I think it has more autonomy than that, and we have to speak to 'the cook' and 'the healer' and 'the therapist' within. And you allow them to come to the forefront, so that the local ego and it's limiting and habituated structures are pushed aside for the time being. You have other personas and it's who you bring out of the background into the forefront that makes the difference as to how you feel about things. Or, as Francis of Assisi put it, "What we are looking for is who is looking."

Jean seemed to have masterful knowledge of anything and everything... Her take on Jung's archetypes and how the "student practitioner" could actually work with them simply thrilled me. Imagine tapping into an inner psychical "code" or "field of information" as an actual skill set... Delving into this arena was certainly my life's passion for so many reasons... Naturally if we can determine our personal archetype, we're more than halfway down the path of "knowing thyself", knowing the Daimon of our soul, our true genius, and perhaps more importantly, knowing thyself as a bridge to knowing God.

I'd been "working" with Archetypes seemingly forever, and because my approach to the Tarot is Jungian, I've done much study in the area. Downloads from their "field of information" come easily at this point... But Jean Houston's mentorship on the subject far surpassed my take on it all.

There was always a brilliant twist or... a deeper value to what one might have been privy to before when it came to just about everything. And as a result, there was the experience of remarkable expansion through her lessons and the exercises that were inevitably meant to heighten the senses, and indeed develop one's capacity for higher consciousness! In fact, a cornerstone in Jean's mentorship was the introduction to what could be thought of as the higher self... Or something like the higher self... A palpable, cosmically expanded version of it, as far as I'm concerned.

I'd like to share her explanation of what she refers to as "The Entelechy". Of course, you should know, Jean's in-person introduction to it is more powerful than I can say... but what I can say is that "knowing my Entelechy" has been life changing enough for me to share what is available to me about it.

I should start with this: With the connection to one's own Entelechy, one enters the state of flow and true coherence...

The dictionary definition is: "Entelechy is a vital force that directs an organism toward self-fulfillment"

This is how Jean describes it:

"Entelechy is a word that Aristotle used to describe higher guidance and purpose. It is the entelechy of an acorn to be an oak, of a baby to be a grown-up human being. Contact entelechy and all circuits are "go". Tune to it and another order of perspective is at hand, one that comprehends the spatial and the temporal, that lifts the Earth of one's seeing into another domain where love rules and the patterns of higher governance are known. Words cannot really describe it. Metaphors fritter and fry in the fires of analogy. Entelechy is known in its experience. It is being in the flow. It is cooking on more burners. It is making the highest use of skills one has acquired. It is putting old capacities to work in new ways and discovering capabilities we never knew we had. It is growing the evolutionary organs of our future,

transcendent selves. *When we live in service to our entelechy, we comprehend the genius of Leonardo, the compassion of Buddha, the social consciousness of Martin Luther King, the word craft of Emily Dickinson. We become actors on the stage of a new story, our personal play a scene in the sacred drama of all times and places. We experience profound joy, a sense of blissful felicity. We enter the domains of the mythic and come face to face with the fullness of what we are."*

I was evidently meant to know Jean... Indeed, she was a vital member of my Heroine's journey... For one thing, I certainly met my match when it came to passionately experiencing life itself as a grand mythic adventure... I have been blessed to know her and to have learned so very much from her.

The final yet ongoing study of the many parts of the Human psyche that I've engaged in for some time now, is called, "Voice Dialogue". This is an entire approach to inner work that literally utilizes the multitudes within... The polyphrenic team within as Jean might say... And for me this methodology feels like the culmination of so much of the work I've engaged in over the years.

I was lucky enough to find an amazing teacher in the field right here in Boulder... And she just happens to be the daughter of the man who originated the methodology. When life "falls into place" so perfectly, you naturally had better follow its lead. Tamar Stone is not only an incredibly gifted teacher but I'm certain she's considered a true gift to any and all who have studied with her.

In my own healing arts practice, by this time I had many tools and methodologies at my disposal, depending upon individual needs.

And it is true that sometimes people seem to wonder why I had so many interests and areas of study. But as far as I'm concerned, they fit together rather brilliantly... Anyway, I've lived a long life. Why wouldn't I engage in its many riches. Once upon a time I worried I might be considered little more than a "Jack of all trades and a master of none." But this is a terrible cultural judgement of many who's Souls were meant for the path of a Renaissance woman or man. I suppose I came to splendid terms with this notion in these... Renaissance times.

4

ENDLESS TIME, THE FINAL STORY

We are mythic beings...
Our story fills us, holds our dreams,
our meaning, our destiny,
and the seeds of our unfolding.
At the same time,
time is ever so much more
than what we are able to grasp
"in the moment".
Yet each moment
holds all time nonetheless.
If we think creatively enough,
we just might find a piece of eternity.
The child within does well
to take the hand of the wise woman
for we are all ages in one.

Erica Sarzin-Borrillo

I don't know how many more stories are left in me. This will be one of the last in this book... the end, fini... And yet the story itself has no sense of finality. No... because it's the story of endless time, actually. It's the story of the very first time I experienced simultaneous time as a little girl, and how I return to that moment of simultaneous time many times over.

Perhaps the memory keeps my eternal child eternal but it also re-aligns me with an existential gestalt in my psyche and my heart. Whatever it's worth, it certainly made a profound impression on me at age what... 7?

Granted, I already had "heightened" experiences where the subtlest things most adults, let alone children would never have noticed, but they had radical meaning to me. This experience felt mythic and at such a young age!

My mother and stepfather would often take me on their trips to NYC for their philately shows at the armory. It was a family affair as we'd meet up with Mado and Papa Sam. Anyway, it was a trip we'd take often.

I'm remembering now however, being in the back seat of our BMW sedan with its tan leather seats. I don't quite know why it's important for me to recall that car except to say my wildly imaginative mind is suddenly transforming it into a time machine; a chariot that brought me to some apparent altered state... Because when we parked and I stepped out of that car, into the garage, I felt my very first full-on sensation of "I've been here before!"

Now, if indeed this was Dejá vu and no more than a trick of the mind... a timing glitch in the brain, believe me, my interpretation was never going to be as prosaic as that. This was yet one more HG Wells moment in time that sent me to the heart of the Cosmos and back again. Not only had "I been there" before, I knew I'd been everywhere before, and many times over. And the vastness of time itself moved me to tears. I stood in the middle of that parking lot and became hysterical. I wept from the bottom of my heart and never forgot that moment in time that held all time.

I remember how my mother laughed at me, knowing of matters like Dejá Vu. But for me this was just one more entry point to... to the larger world... the much larger world.

Now, I've lived with this story my whole life long. And I admit, I either "allowed it" its own psychic power, or it was simply my "style" to perceive, or filter such experiences through some kind of Universal consciousness... I suppose this was the lens I was born with. Call it creative thinking, mystical, magical, out there, or crazy... I know I stumbled upon the mystery of time present, time past, and time future... And I came upon it through an experience in an underground garage a long long time ago. Look, what do any of us really know outside of science, and even then... Yes, even then life itself is like the Japanese story of Rashomon. Everything can be left to inter-pretation. In fact, as I write this, I'm reminded of my playwriting days at the Mime Theatre. The most difficult writing was abstraction for the simple reason that it's human instinct to create a linear narrative to what is put before one's eyes... and abstraction can elicit a whole variety of unique stories in much the same way as Rorschach! But that's life! And the implications are wild when you think about it... For me personally, I've had a lifetime being me, and as "out there" as my ex-periences have been, they are the ones that have filled me with aliveness and have actually allowed for a remarkable interplay with "the Universe". Whether we filter things "accurately" or not, we're nonetheless in a conversation with life. I just have come to realize over the years that the conversation includes the Cosmos itself! And if we listen well, we'll hear the sound of our own calling... Not once, but through our lives... quite possibly from the past, the present, and maybe even the future! So, maybe life is one big Abstraction, but whatever appears before us, may ultimately be the gifts, the symbols and the metaphors of our personal coding...

I was an artist and something of a mystic from the beginning. How could I not have interpreted my experience that day, as I did? And how could I not have used it in creative visualizations when so much of the time it appeared as some sort of psychic backdrop or wallpaper in my mind?

Years later, it became integral to a large intension I wanted more than anything to fulfill. I always regretted that I didn't. I did feel the teaching of simultaneous time on some level was part of my destiny. Perhaps the telling of the story many times over was enough... or merely speaking of it here, on the page, dear Reader, will inspire what it was meant to...

But still, I tend to think the story is not quite over... Perhaps the more mature me needed to and still needs to collaborate with that 7-year-old and make something more of that moment in time that held all time...

I'll explain; I always thought one day I'd unpack my experience of simultaneous time and utilize it somehow, because the thrill of it stuck... and had relevance in my opinion. I believe there's been reason for its central focus in my life, certainly along with all my passions of which there have been many of course... But you see, coalescence generally means the inner weaver of one's lifetime steps up to destiny and by age 60, that was taking place.

That was right around the time I met Jean. So many reasons brought me to her, but little did I know that eventually I'd find a way through her to further explore my 7-year old's fascination with Time... and how to use it with intentionality. Interestingly enough what I quickly learned once I started working with Jean was that her great passion was Time as well... And she too had a remarkable childhood experience of it that opened up fields of lifetime study and practices. We never discussed this personally but this seemed one more point of commonality, so naturally something intriguing was bound to come of it.

Since much of Jean's way of teaching was through guided med-itation and body/mind exercises there was always the possibility of mind/body transformation. And there was the greater possibility of manifesting one's higher intentions by working in "the imaginal realm"...

There was one such area of practice that kept turning up in Jean's on-line courses, retreats, and Salons. I tinkered with it for a while till I finally made sense of it for my life. Like almost any and all practices, rituals, or theories, when one infuses them with creativity and passion, they can be amazingly powerful. This became such a practice for me... and certainly led to some wildly creative thinking, that's for sure. I warn you ahead of time.

This exercise was called the Terma. The Terma originally comes from the Tibetan Buddhist monks who spoke of the "Hidden Treasure" or hidden teachings of their religious traditions. When I recently looked into the Tibetan practice, I was astounded to learn that their concept of the Terma actually referred to a time capsule, hidden for the sake of future generations. They were also thought to be a kind of "mind treasure" or "pure vision".

I don't frankly know what Jean's process was when she came up with her Terma practice but it had to have been based on the Tibetan notion of the Hidden Treasure and the Time capsule. For certain, her practice was meant to guide the practitioner into creating an intention (with "pure vision") for whatever you wished for through co-creation with the Universe!

Of course, any manifestation practice does require pure vision and belief… I think it also requires fierce dreaming. I also think we'd all do well when working in this way, to "fiercely envision" our highest dream, one that has to do with our best intentions for the world. One that can see beyond the tragic nature of the world's woes of which there are many… Jean's Terma practice was designed to dream a possibility into a probability.

I will put it simply. My higher vision, though it's perhaps too large to put to the test, has always been Human coalescence and Unity Consciousness… I do my very best to stay true to a greater vision of that "Divine Feminine" through whatever means I have at my disposal. I have to believe that the thread of my life as an artist has some meaning in this context… Yes, if we were "born to these times" our gifts are the tools of our destiny.

All this being said, it's not always easy to hold the passion and the hope when the world is falling apart. Perhaps the hope, passion, and original dream can still remain vibrant within our personal Terma! What a beautiful thought.

I love the Tibetan notion of the time capsule. Naturally it would appeal to the 7-year-old who forevermore will believe in eternity and simultaneous time and the power of the imaginal realm… She's forever alive even when I'm not fully. Jean Houston's Terma exercise brought me back to my younger self, and our experience of simultaneous time.

In my mind's eye, I see myself hand-in-hand with that little girl who once was, as we gaze upon a patch of earth right outside the parking lot. And somehow, we had the inner knowing this was the site of some hidden treasure... perhaps a treasure we ourselves had buried long ago... perhaps lifetimes ago... Here lay the time capsule so full of teachings from God knows where... And of course, my higher dreams...my greater intentions... my Terma.

Now Jean's highly imaginative exercise was directed differently than how mine went, I admit... but the potency of the intentionality was very much in place... Jean directed folks to imagine burying their personal termas, with their personal intention sometime in their childhood and later found in the present. I know someone who imagines her lifetime terma buried presently in her backyard where she's able to revisit it, and re-envision the intention...

Of course, the burial site of simultaneous time changes things up but makes the outcome of the intention far more powerful to me... I mean, just imagine unpacking a treasure full of radiant intention and sending it forth through simultaneous time... through time and space... and through the quantum Universe... Talk about fierce dreaming! I will also say this; I truly believe the collaboration if you will, between my 7-year-old mystic in the making and the elder I've become, as giving a greater passion and amplification to the terma and all it implies... James Hillman says, "Stay with the image"... If it possesses you, that may be all that matters... It may not even need be grounded or acted upon. I recall one of my early intentions happened to be a "destiny project" I'd placed inside my time capsule... It was a nearly whole baked Ted Talks theatre piece about "The Divine Feminine"... and the piece opened with me reaching into "the earth" for a "Hidden Treasure" full of radiance and imagery of the divine! There is no doubt in my mind, had I followed through this could have been one wildly beautiful and informative performance art piece... I couldn't do it. I had to let go and simply "hold the image" as Hillman would say. I happen to think my Terma has actually been working on many levels though...

I mean, where does our "gnostic knowing" actually come from, the wisdom of the ages... the psychic sense of it all. Naturally it comes from oh so many places with so many ways to think on it... perhaps the whole shebang from the beginning of time exists within our DNA, past lives, parallel lives, the creative unconscious, the quantum fields, archetypal patterns, etc. etc. etc. There are many roads that can open the mind to higher consciousness and much that can inspire radical awakening.

But perhaps what thrills me most about the notion of the Buddhist's "Terma" is the metaphor itself... Maybe it appeals to the Romantic in me. But ultimately I see "The Hidden Treasure" as the brilliant gem that radiates from deep within our very Soul. Therein lies the radiance we're forever chasing... and the eternal flame that shines bright through time past, time present, and time future. With this in mind, one has to wonder how in Heaven's name we ever lost sight of our greatest treasure of all... ourselves...

I think what this all really means... is that quite possibly all things are actually possible. I know this to be true, because a little 7-year-old girl keeps reminding me of that vitally important truth!

5

TIME PRESENT...
JOURNALS FROM THE DESCENT

"Quiet friend who has come so far,
feel how your breathing
makes more space around you.
Let this darkness be a bell tower
and you the bell.
As you ring, what batters you
becomes your strength.
Move back and forth into the change.
What is it like, such intensity of pain?
If the drink is bitter, turn yourself into wine.
In this uncontainable night,
be the mystery at the crossroads of your senses,
the meaning discovered there.
And if the World has ceased to hear you,
say to the silent earth: I flow.
To the rushing water, speak: I am."

Rainer Maria Rilke
from *The Sonnets to Orpheus II*

Has there ever been a year like 2020? Oh, Goddess! I have been journaling here and there while in quarantine… and as I'd stated from the start of this book, my own heart problems were already serious… But it was not easy to say the least, to return to the writing once those heart issues became as extreme as they did… with juxtaposition to the global pandemic. I have questioned whether my family history could have meaning in the face of a crises we've never seen the likes of, and that would no doubt take more lives than could ever have been imagined… But then I myself, like others at this time have little choice but to follow the thread of my inner battle towards meaning. And so, I continued to write the stories of ancestors, my childhood, my philosophical musings, my mytho-poetic essays, my channeled messages from spirit and soul… and of course images of the art I've created over time…

Here, in this final chapter however, I shall make an attempt to describe the present moment which has brought us all together yet shattered us at the same time… I begin with my heart…

March 2020 somewhere around the middle of the month…

I hardly know what to say… I live in fear because of the wild drama that has brought so much change in the world and in my health. And of course, the cross over symptoms between the two are uncanny… I live with outrageous shortness of breath and labored breathing, which of course is the hallmark of this devastating virus and so it has been confusing.

I've always said that even on my deathbed I will still manage to create beauty… I'll be painting or writing because I live and breathe creativity… Isn't it interesting though, that now, I can barely breathe the air around me, let alone creativity, beauty, or ecstasy. And just the other day, I was diagnosed with Emphysema of all things. What? How? How did I develop COPD overnight? And is this true? The last CT scan revealed "a little pneumonia"… It's all so suspicious… but just to note, I am devastatingly ill at the worst time in history. And I will say this: The Black Plague was more romantic. On a personal level; everything seems dead set against me getting well. And I feel like my "indomitable spirit "is pushing hard in efforts to harness some chi…

Unfortunately, the Devil himself seems to be pushing back harder. Harder than the Angel of Death would ever have to if he was the one in charge here! Perhaps the notion comes from my romantic view of such things… But listen to this mysterious synchronicity… About a week before I got sent to the ER (March 12) a most tragic loss was experienced by all those who knew and adored the magnificent Peter Saide. When I learned of his death, I wailed. I simply couldn't fathom it. This happened about 2 weeks before the Corona virus made its way over to the US. But his death had nothing to do with the virus.

Poor beautiful Peter died of an embolism to his heart after he had gone through back surgery. He was mourned worldwide. Here's the synchronicity… I'd known Peter through a play I'd done with him called, "Death Takes a Holiday"… He played death; a romantic, almost angelic archetype, who wanted to learn of the human experience and so he slipped into the body of a dying Prince and halted all death throughout the land while "on vacation". The tale is actually a beautiful love story between Death and the dying girl he'd fallen in love with at first sight… Eventually he would have to "escort her to the other side"… because of course death is inevitable… When together they left the land of the living, balance was restored and with it, the final frontier, death. My experience of this beautiful play was simply wonderful… One of my favorites. I adored the cast, and the magnificence of our lead, Peter Saide.

Three years have passed and this beautiful man, at 36, so full of life dies from a blood clot. It was a devastating loss. Not long after, I had a dream about him. I actually dreamed he came for me on my deathbed. He sat by me and smiled… And upon seeing his eyes, I was calmed at once by his countenance… He reached out to take my hand and I knew all was well, because as in the play, he was my loving usher.

I wish I could say I've remained calm in the face of what has followed me since. My personal health crises interfacing with this global plague is far too much to bear. And truthfully, the timing of Peter's passing is oddly synchronistic because indeed, since then, the number of deaths "throughout the land" has been apocalyptic in nature… So very very strange.

In any event, as far as my personal story is concerned, I had been doing well at least for a while… stabilizing on the drugs for my A-fib and ventricular tachycardia… or shall I say I was doing well enough to continue writing this book, when I got cut down at the knees and wound up in the hospital with major internal bleeding that required surgery. I had even gotten the go-ahead to vacation for a week in Mexico. The plan was to get more aggressive with the treatment in March when I returned. But that was not to be. Hell broke loose in my body the day we returned to the US. I remember feeling poorly when I woke that morning. I was having difficulty breathing and had that terrible feeling I might pass out at any moment. The trip back was even worse as I developed extreme edema... I couldn't imagine what had gone wrong but did have a hunch it had something to do with the prescription of blood thinners I'd picked up from the pharmacy... You see, I'd been on samples but the night before had started the prescription. I couldn't quite believe there would be a difference so I continued to take the new pills for about 5 more days... But I was getting sicker and sicker. It occurred to me that the samples and the prescription might have been manufactured differently or elsewhere... To be honest it felt like I'd gotten a bad batch... or lot...It actually felt like it was a much higher dose... I finally decided to go to my pharmacy and explain what was going on... because honestly, I had no choice but to experiment (despite the cost) and purchase another prescription and pray for the best. Well, indeed, it had apparently been my bad luck to randomly get that bad batch... because the new one was perfectly fine... Incredible, yes? Well, I continued to take the new meds... All seemed well for a few days... My terrible symptoms went away and I felt exceedingly relieved... until the next set of symptoms brought me to the emergency room... just a few days later... And I really must say I wonder if any of this had anything at all to do with those 5 days worth of the bad batch!

This is how it all went. By now, we were becoming more and more aware of the spreading of the Covid-19 virus... I developed a low-grade fever, horrendous pain that wrapped around my belly to my back, and some pretty hefty GI trouble... When I spoke with the triage nurse from my doctor's office, she told me to get to an ER for covid test screening just to be on the safe side. Well, I was at the ER for hours and never got screened for the test but was horrified to learn what they'd found on my cat scan. I was internally bleeding... because of the blood thinners! Yes! I had "multiple left retroperitoneal hematomas" and active bleeding which would necessitate surgery or an "IR non neuro embolization".

Emergency after emergency seems to be the way of my life these days... but after having had a lifetime of Lyme flare ups I've come to understand that the serious nature of my heart disease will not easily see me through without meds or procedures any longer... despite my profound sensitivities to drugs... as proven by the hemorrhage on the blood thinners... (the so called gold star blood thinner). So I was rushed from the stand alone ER via ambulance to Anschutz Medical Center, where their ER docs were waiting for me. There was nothing lackadaisical about their efforts with me despite the fact that the hospital was filled already with so many fallen ill... including those with overt signs of Covid-19.

From the moment I was greeted there on March 12 to when I left on the 14th, I had more blood taken than imaginable. No one felt I had the virus though despite my fever and a chest Xray that indicated "a little pneumonia". This was all about the hemorrhage and my heart. In fact, they sent a surgeon down to me to make sure I fully understood how serious this was. I've been through quite a few near-death experiences as of late but they do seem to be escalating... as if the gravity of my personal story has a mythic counterpart with the global health crises... Nonetheless, according to the docs at Anschutz, a major hemogram of this kind was no small matter and the implications would complicate my heart issues forever more... They also indicated that this was an emergency far worse than the virus at hand... The word at the time was that most people would get over Covid... I'm not so certain it remains the truth because 3 weeks later the extreme nature of this pandemic has already devastated the globe... And I admit, I was lucky to have had that emergency then as opposed to now. They did save my life... and I'm still here typing away. What's to come of course brings me back to those sweet lyrics my mother would sing to me; "Que sera sera... Whatever will be will be..."

So, I had the surgery and made it through, but crises has become a way of life, with several emergencies since, drug reactions that have uncanny cross over symptoms with the Covid, and a new diagnosis of Emphysema. I'd hoped I'd return home to convalesce and be back on my feet but alas, that has not been the case... and whatever "procedures" or surgeries may logically come into play for me, my terribly complicated health condition is raging at the worst time in history... and both crises are getting worse and worse by the minute... I have been dealing with dramatic symptoms with alarmed doctors stating I have no more time to play around without treatment... and by treatment they do mean surgery... I've come to understand that I'm clearly between a rock and a hard place but have accepted as best I can to follow through with a very risky procedure called "The Lariat". According to my doc, it is necessary and my only choice... and so they will try to schedule it sometime in May, that is, if the pandemic deems it safe enough to even be in a hospital... let alone have surgery... As for the risky part of this story is concerned, it would seem that life itself is risky business at this time... The Lariat is rarely done anymore because of the risk factor and only for "compassion cases" like mine... So, I'm definitely afraid for my life... and this is no existential matter... As my doctors say, "This is real".

But so is Covid-19... This pandemic is ever so real, though it still feels surreal... And look, clearly, I am but one soul amongst millions afraid for their lives and livelihood. Our country has the highest case rate... possibly the highest death rate and is in grave danger of collapsing on every level simultaneously... This will go on they say. I will personally experience much more drama... but God only knows what will actually be the fate of the world...

And so... I'd like to speak to this moment in time that seems to go even beyond my personal story... though in reality the moment in time has become our personal story like no other time in history. We are on a collective journey... a collective crucible... or chrysalis at best... and in many ways it is forcing the presence of our soul's needs over our ego's needs... This may be the one true thing we walk away with when the time of Corona has come to an end... tragedies not withstanding... I can only pray we'll emerge transformed... but for now it's hard to escape the madness. I grapple with this now; I never intended to scribe too much of my health dramas as I've indicated because they seem to hold so little hope, and little resource for inspiration... but then again, I'm well aware that our sacred wounds are the essential ingredients to the soul's mythic journey to wholeness... and sharing our vulnerabilities may be an essential factor to the healing of the whole... So... This Covid-19 is indeed our collective sacred wound... It's part of my story as my story is part of the whole...

This will be written in history books... (I pray) But you can take it from me... The global rug has been pulled from beneath our feet... I'm not certain there was ever a single disaster story written or imagined that compares... and of course the world has known of countless wars, atrocities, and holocausts by the hand of man's inhumanity to man...

Nothing compares when the whole of mankind finds itself powerless in the fight against an invisible invader of this sort.

The best of the human spirit is called upon... and our collective vulnerability is remarkably compelling after many years of judgement, prejudice, and in many ways a veering away from the path of the soul...in favor of the path of the market place... I just have to wonder if our path back to matters of the soul will not have been too late... Some might say that fear may be far too negative to be of any use... But as Michael Meade states; fear at its best is a positive... once upon a time meaning; Fare as in thoroughfare... a means to move through... Well, personally I want desperately to move through this plague and come out the other side... because this life, with all its existential flaws is so very beautiful and so worth cultivating... I am journaling through these days while in state wide lockdown... and when I can move beyond my own weakened state, I contemplate as it seems to be my style... Why would it be different now in this intense stage of Human growth... I pray we are ever-evolving, especially at times like these... (Times that seem like end times)

April 9th Journal entry:

We are well into what feels like a death watch... It begins to feel that way what with the world-wide data... We are living a difficult dream and the longer it goes on, the harder it is to believe it will ever feel safe again.

Safety... Safety... My mind wanders back to the recent pages I wrote, of my mother's time in Europe during the war... No one felt safe during the holocaust and I've always marveled how any of them withstood the terrible fear and stress of living under those circumstances... Just a few weeks ago I transcribed my Aunt Billie's unfolding story of Paris burning and how no one could be out in the streets without gas masks. I found it all unimaginable... yet they (my family) took courage under my grandfather's lead and against all odds they fled to America where they found safety and freedom.

I have contemplated and fought in my own way for freedom my whole life. And in fact, freedom was my mother's greatest desire through her life as well. With me, the freedom I sought was perhaps of a more spiritual nature than my mother's, who had been subject to the Nazi regime... And what came with that was a deep-rooted need for safety... In my life I've never truly had to worry for my safety... not really... but now, safety is the impending issue for us all. And I grieve for what we had...

We will have tremendous limitations from now on... with boundary making that does not come naturally to the human spirit... but as one who seeks the soul's freedom, I can only hope we will find the way to the sacred, the divine, and the greater parts within that understand the cosmic way of the soul despite our future restrictions. Higher creativity will be demanded of us for certain and I return to this: It is a spiritual matter as always! May we live in the greater light, one and all!

April 13th. A COVID-19 Nightmare

I was stuck on a mountain trying to "get Home"... waiting for help that never came. On the edge for days on end, I was scaling the mountain terrified I wouldn't make it. I could see for miles below and beyond yet couldn't see around the corner and was frightened by my lack of footing. There was a car on the road far below trying to make its way up the steep incline... and for some reason I thought they were coming to save me but they never did. I was on hazardous ground never knowing what was just ahead...

Down the mountain to my right was a lake and a couple of folks were swimming. Wow! I couldn't believe something playful was going on at such a dangerous time...

When I looked below to my left, I saw that someone had left their backpack and clothing... I couldn't see him but heard yelling from around the corner of the mountain... so I suspected that's where he'd gone... but I just couldn't get to him... I finally figured a way to at least view the scene... It had to be "through someone else's eyes"... it was as if I'd slipped into another body and was no longer on the edge but was inside a "room" or cave within the mountain itself... and was able to see outside to the other side... or... "around the corner" that I'd not been able to see from my prior perspective. In any event, what I was now able to see, seemed to be a scene from another country, and another time! There were Nazis all over the place, tearing and beating people up. One caught my eye through the opening in the cave, and looked up at me with a sneer as if to say, "You're next".

I woke up coughing... I pray I don't have Covid!

April 22... a fb post

Today was the first day I left the house to go grocery shopping. It's been since well before the lockdown but we seriously needed to restock before the next round. Well, our Costco run was surreal. And I have to admit, friends, that I felt a little like I was taking my life in my hands to merely be back in public. (not to mention that the outing felt like I was running a marathon)... Paris is certainly not burning with the residue of war bombs... and though we are not all of us wearing gas masks, we are in masks... (that is most of us are) because the air is contaminated with this deadly virus...

I am slated to have my "risky surgery" as soon as viable. I don't know what that looks like at this point, however. I'm simply using this time to further grow my soul like the rest of us... while praying we will not only land on our feet, but will be blessed by brilliant minds, compassionate souls, and leaders galore. I continue to stay creative... and am trying to learn my lessons in this time of Corona.

April 23rd...

May I have the courage to withstand the hopeless nature of this plague. More importantly, may I draw upon my greater imagination and mythic perspective, hoping I don't by-pass the literal truth of the moment... but perhaps will See, Feel, Live, and Manifest the higher truth of the moment... knowing the higher truth holds endless possibility, born of the eternal mystery, that is no doubt filled with miracle after miracle!!!!!!!

It has been hard and I hold both ends of my human but ever-loving mystical side. Is it possible to live in the ecstatic plain, and in the raw vulnerability of the underworld simultaneously? My God, I feel I'm running naked betwixt and between both worlds... I guess I've always been one to "Feel" both with my heart of hearts... Someone asked me the other day if I was in good spirits, and I responded with, "I am in ALL spirits"... As I've said many times before, to quote the great Walt Whitman, "I am multitudes". I suppose Whitman and I are Jungian at heart... and this is the way of my soul... I thank God, I can still find the ecstatic when the ground we walk these days has suddenly come to look like Hades Town... It's up to us somehow to take up the lute like Orpheus and sing our souls to the light within the darkness. And so, it is... and so, it is... and so it is...

April 27 Dream of Gaia

I have had a few dreams lately that have stayed with me through the days... This one I consider a gift and reminder of my very being that refuses to fade away amidst these troubled times...

I suppose this dream reveals the beauty seeker in me... but more... I suppose I needed this dream. I needed to embody this potent medicine that is... how do I say this; the perfectly resonant medicine of my soul... the stuff of the natural world, if that makes sense... I was in the woods... the Northeast woods. I came upon a house that was perfectly nestled by mother Nature and when I saw it, I stood breathless before it's beauty. And in fact, my feeling was one of a powerful resonance. I felt it was my Home. But then you see I spent much of my childhood playing in those woods and later by the ocean... There's a part of me that grieves for the intimacy I had with my surroundings and place of birth. In any event, I was there once more in my dream. I opened the door to the house in the woods and went upstairs to the kitchen and witnessed a most unusual sight. In the kitchen on one of the walls were two enormous wooden sculptures carved from tree trunks. They were massive pieces that took up the entire wall and jutted through the ceiling. I then proceeded to tour the rest of the house and found that every room was as magnificent as the next because of their amazingly natural and organic look. Everything was designed to bring mother Nature into the home... And I had to wonder who the architect was... And then of course I realized it was me. I was the creator of this Home... It came out of my imagination... my dream... and had something to do at least metaphorically with my purpose in life. When I walked all the way through the House, the walls opened up and I found myself outside and back by the mill pond where my own mother would take me as a child. And if it's possible to feel deeper and deeper layers of what it means to be Home, this feeling was the epitome of it.

When I woke, that feeling came with me... but with as well, a sense of absolute oneness with Nature. Yes, I was brought back to my inherent childhood understanding of that oneness... The cognizance of true Nature within our souls is ultimately what is needed. And perhaps it's become more subconscious than I'd like, but nonetheless I know it has driven me in almost everything I reach for as an artist and a woman. I do believe the old phrase, "We've got to get back to the Garden" is no doubt more important than generally understood anymore, as our focus is less than natural. But this dream was a gift from the God's and perhaps a kind of metaphysical realignment that I needed to remind me of the good authentic life. The way I see it, the reconnection to nature, and EVERYTHING that means… everything… is the World work… and such work is part of one's tapestry… the woven threads of one's life…

I hope to remember this, and indeed, I hope to remember the ways in which I've been blessed despite crisis and drama, or perhaps because of them. I would like to think that our so-called tragedies have purpose and even the darkest angel has our best interest in mind. This is a quote from one of my favorite plays called Lucifer's Child:

"I have always believed that life demands of us that we love it, not merely certain sides of it and not only one's own ideas and ideals, but life itself in all its forms before it will give us anything in return. I could not therefore see myself for long in any tragic light. All my life I have joyfully clung to the dark angel." Life is beautiful…

Late July 2020

So much has happened since my last entry. Like much of what has been felt by most these days, we seem to be suspended in time while waiting "for things to get better". And while waiting, we're all of us attempting to "buck up" and hold our heads high. Never before has my duality presented such a chasm.

Even when life seems somewhat harmonious, the big trick is to be fully present to its Sacred nature, with the help of some kind of spiritual ritual employed daily.

But now, the pandemic is completely limiting our sense of free spirit and connection to our fellow man. And the fracturing within our precious American government is forcing us to live with the unthinkable: corruption and propaganda. (something I never dreamt possible having been a child of the 50's in the land of free… at least by comparison to Nazi Germany)

This chaos holds no sense of possible coherence in the near future!

Fierce dreaming takes hutzpah, that's for sure! I'll get there, friends, I promise. And I pray you do too. At times like this, I thank God for our multitudes. We need to be calling on our fiercest inner magic makers, because miracles are needed now more than ever before.

Early August

How could I make entries? I've been unfaithful to these morning pages as I've not been entirely present to my seemingly random feelings amidst the times... Racism, protesting, violence in the streets, 180,000 deaths in our country, 822,000 globally... With no end in sight... With no end in sight... with no compassion from the top... but only a lack of empathetic leadership so vitally needed!

I dreamt of a new paradigm. I assumed we'd see its miraculous effects by now. But it seems like the Soul of all has let go of every woven thread it had ever held within itself from the beginning of time!

On top of it all, on the personal level, my health is worse than ever. I had the bleed in March which required surgery... and had more surgery in June (lariat) to prevent a stroke. I suppose I should be grateful to know I'm safe from such a fate but the surgery did weaken my heart further and has left me with an inflammatory condition and excruciating pain.

Does the "down side" of my duality show? Of course, it does. I am made of shadow and light. Yes, my eye is on the sparrow forever more because the Visionary within is just that stubborn... But don't believe what they say; that opposites can't hold the same space... that hope cannot survive as long as we feel the blues, so to speak... hope often resides side by side with the wound... which would mean with the actual suffering... oh yes indeed...

We need the music of the spheres to heal the world... To bring Love and Coherence back to Humanity, to mother Earth, to the Cosmos, and maybe even back to the Gods and Goddesses themselves. Play the melody again, oh Muse. Play a good song for Peace on Earth!

Mid-August 2020

I feel compelled to speak of our greater story, my "duality" notwithstanding. I don't know where things will lead as the world is not only processing the time of Corona, but living in the Time of the Tower...

Anyway, I will say it, whether this book gets published or not...

Of course, I stand for the uniqueness of the pathless path and the individual journey. But as I've said so many times before, my strongest stance is for the "One and The Many". In the end, our individual journey becomes that much more potent in partnership and collaboration.

I'm thinking now of the ancient Greek aphorism "know thyself"... In its purest form it indicates that "man must stand and live according to his nature". Naturally without Self-knowledge one can't hope to "become Oneself" fully and wholly. But there's more to this age-old idea that strikes me as it pertains to Unity consciousnesses. This is the way I see it... and, this is the way I hope it plays out in the Human adventure, individually and collectively... We come in barely conscious, and spend our early years developing ourselves along with our personal ego and persona... Through our lives we dive more deeply into our interior psyche or more externally depending upon our own Soul's style, I suppose... But I think that "knowing thyself" comes with the Self-knowledge that WE are in this together... We are truly the world, as the saying goes... I think it's part of our destiny individually and collectively to grow towards this way of being but it's a tough paradigm to ground, isn't it? And then of course there really is ever so much more to the continuous journey to self discovery, because in the end, "knowing thyself" in every way would open the portal to the embodiment of the Divine... In the highest, for each and every one us, "I am that I am". I believe the amalgam of all three is the ideal. Herein lies our Human potential. Perhaps "the new paradigm" we've been reaching so fervently for is simply this: the manifestation of that amalgam which happens to be the gist of The Divine Feminine itself!

I'm thinking of the final archetype from the Tarot; "The World", and how it fits in with this spiritual possibility even at this late date... I'm trying to meditate upon it... at this late date.

Cathy McClellan's "World" from her "Star Tarot" brilliantly tells the tale of genuine wholeness, integration, and Unity consciousness...

The image is that of a Goddess holding the entire world. I like to think of her as The Great mother, or perhaps the epitome of the Divine Feminine... The One who holds the whole of Humanity with the Highest form of understanding and compassion. She is the archetype within and without who blends paradox after paradox. She blends the shadow and the light. She blends the opposites, and is even able to see the ego of the World without disdain... and does so, like a master alchemist.

And here's her beauty; if you take a second look at this World card, this Goddess, this Great mother, this Divine Feminine, you will find her to be in a state of Divine fertility. And what is she ready to birth but the greater possibility of a new dawn...

I honestly believe the finer part of the Human psyche will always dream a greater dream. But if we can somehow live out our mutual destiny to not only grow ourselves but grow the World, then we will have answered the wishes of the Gods themselves. Perhaps in this sense, we were meant to be the midwives of new and finer paradigms. Times have been tough as of late and perhaps they will get tougher. But if it is true that "we were born to these times", then we surely cannot afford to take our eyes off the sparrow. We must dream with an undying passion, for ours is the story of initiation, awakening and hopefully transformation in the face of the most challenging moments in history."

Sept. 6

I will journal till the end... whatever "the end" means. Mythically speaking, as Michael Meade suggests, the world will never die. But the times, though they may intend re-creation, are full of destruction as well. And we are doing our best to withstand the energy of the Goddess Kali... (and maybe use that energy to ultimately heal our predicament) When I try to imagine what she may be trying to say to humanity, I come up with this: "It is time, dear Ones, to surrender the ego... let go the fight... let go the power play. let go the old out-moded paradigm now and forevermore! And finally manifest the love you claim to hold within your hearts!"

September 18th

I'm thinking this morning of my Terma, and visualizing a collective prayer. It seems the perfect moment in time to dig for the sacred intention that lies deep within "our hidden treasure". Its power is surely needed now in this time of COVID, global warming, political chaos, and Universal descent. Might as well intend from the inner team of Magical Visionaries is what I say! It might be the only way to truly bring this world back into alignment and radiance!

I just have to say, however, that it wasn't so long ago when many of us were feeling that radiance in palpable terms in what largely felt like a collective awakening... A quickening... And now of course it seems the world has flipped upside down... But then, I can't help but muse over the idea that maybe, just maybe the natural order of creation really is collapse and renewal... And boy oh boy, aren't we ever in the thick of it!

What I do know is this: if the world was on a great voyage towards Unity once upon a time, then our awakening couldn't have been for naught...

Oct. 21

It seems I've dedicated my life to Beauty...

Yes, like Leonard Cohen's beautiful song, I too have "Come so far for Beauty"... But maybe that's the underlying style of many an artist. Certainly, by now, dear reader, you've seen how this theme has run through these memoirs...

However, there's a global tragedy going on at this present time. And suddenly beauty seems to be taking a back seat to the death and dying of our country, our planet, and the strivings of the individual.

It feels so dire, that the very Holy ground I believed to be solid through my life is no longer dependable. I begin to wonder what "my people" felt like during the Holocaust as their sense of power was stripped away by madness.

I suppose we're managing in this "liminal time" but we've entered an unholy paradigm with no knowledge of what's to come.

Maybe we needed to relinquish our controlling nature to some degree, but it may be too hard to bear. And why? Because power play has been the way of the world for so long now that trust in a future that has no face is near impossible, especially when the whole of Humanity is at such odds. I'll never forget one of the letters sent to me by my cousin André regarding the plight of my mother's family... He spoke of the extraordinary time in Europe during the war as "Hitler madness".

Well, there is madness here in America under another's regime and I pray one day we can heal and be whole.

Unfortunately, the madness goes even further now. It is everywhere and on many levels. And it seems to be manifesting in a global nervous breakdown!

I'm trying to trust. I'm trying to stand on the ground of "loving what is". But we are all of us being challenged beyond any drama we've ever known.

I call for you now Beauty…

"Beauty, Beauty, Beauty!"

Oct.23

What an extraordinary time in American history! We are living in an age where what we once relied on as collective truth, has fallen away. I worry about the undying belief in wild storytelling. In the face of American madness, I feel all I can do is try to stay rational and speak my truth, even if it is not agreeable to some.

Divine One, if ever we needed you, we need you now!

Oct. 24

I woke this morning recalling a wonderful poem I learned of through Jean. It is indeed so fitting for the times. I just felt the need to share it now. It's called, "A Sleep of Prisoners" by Christopher Fry.

> *The Human heart can go to the lengths of God…*
> *Dark and cold we may be, but this is no winter now.*
> *The frozen misery of centuries breaks, cracks, begins to move;*
> *The thunder is the thunder of the floes, the thaw, the upstart Spring.*
> *Thank God our time is now when wrong comes up to face us everywhere.*
> *Never to leave us till we take the longest stride of Soul we ever took.*
> *Affairs are now Soul size. The enterprise is exploration into God.*
> *Where are you making for? It takes so many thousand years to wake,*
> *But will you wake for pity sake!*

Oct. 25

"Thank God our time is now when wrong comes up to face us everywhere!" I've been contemplating the wrongs coming up in the world… Haven't we all? And I've been contemplating mine as well. There's so much I haven't spoken of in these memoirs. While I've grown and grown towards some form of enlightenment and service to the world, these dark days bring up… some demons… I'm not entirely certain it's just my inner critic gone haywire.

Some of my losses I finally have to take responsibility for... at least to some degree. I don't know what good it will do now to journal it for all to see but I am sad I wasn't wise enough to give what was needed in the moment... It's hard to be Human, isn't it?

Now that we are isolated from friends and family due to this terrible plague, we all have time on our hands to think how we might do better with each other. I remember going to a weekend retreat that addressed the darkest side of human kind... the stuff within each and every one of us that is simply not kind. It was called Big Mind/Big Heart... a methodology designed by a Buddhist by the name of Genpo Roshi. I wish we could all take the course... especially now during these days of uncertainty.

Our affairs are certainly Soul size, for pity sake!

Oct 26

They say we artists, poets, and storytellers write but one tale in variant through our lives. We try to take a stance for our spiritual issues over and over again whether we know it or not. I say the same goes for all men from the beginning of time... There may be a thousand stories to tell with a thousand narratives... But we're all standing for the Human dilemma... The content is the same...

Freedom...... Truth...... Justice...... Love......

November 11

I have much to say. It's been a rough week.

I had a Birthday... We had an election. The pandemic is 5 times worse than the height of it's first peak and becoming catastrophic. I had to have my 5th test and have been sick for awhile now. I await the results.

Now this: The questions I am left with since my last entry feel larger than ever and why? Because the last 4 years have come to a head so epically that I'm sure Humanity is questioning Humanity. History will look back as will playwrights and perhaps philosophers.

There was an election and the results brought people to the streets with rapture and relief... Joe Biden won! And frankly most of us in America felt the Gods had blessed us with a true Hero... a Hero for the times... one with Grace and a love of the people... unlike the Hitlers of the world... and the likes of Dictators.

But it has all played out like a morality tale. And it is not over. Apparently fierce dreaming is not enough. There will be no peaceful transition by our mad president who is claiming voter fraud and full-blown thievery... We knew there would be shenanigans but never imagined the ego of an American president could possibly go so far as to incite a coup. But of course his devotees are fervent believers who naturely cannot veer from a mindset evidently born long ago.

The first blow for most of us in America was the shocking realization of the sheer size of his following. I don't know that we'll ever be comfortable with the evidently immense split in the so-called United States... The emotions are running high to low and back again almost as if the world has gone bipolar!

My Birthday was November 3rd. And my 69th birthday did deliver the incredible gift of a new administration but with a resistance never seen before in this country. I'm losing track of the timing as it is 8 days after the election but I believe it was the day after Biden was announced President Elect that our current President held an alarming press conference. There was no concession speech as is the Democratic way. Instead, Biden was denounced and it was announced that he had stolen the election.

Since then, Hell has broken loose. And I, like so many others are grieving for what should have been the glorious experience of this transition: pure joy and triumph! But honestly, the spector of the big lie has hung like a dark cloud and no doubt will continue to derail our hold on right and wrong... or truth.

All this cuts like a knife into my life long issue and trigger: Injustice! Many of us are feeling it along with the danger we might very well have to face as the result of the essential forward movement of the new administration being virtually blocked and disabled...

Four years ago, we suspected this man's values were right out of the Fascist's playbook. But who could have seen this coming?.

Perhaps the new paradigm has actually arrived and before our eyes, is in a kind of face off with the epitome of the old paradigm. Indeed, there is a morality tale come to a head in 2020, and he who walks away with the next 4 years of presidency will reveal the birth of grace and Unity... or the continuing push of dominance and Narcissism!

I've been thinking lately of my family during the Holocaust. And I've been thinking quite a bit about Anne Frank and the final words she wrote in her journal. These I can wholeheartedly mirror: "I am a bundle of contradictions. I'm split in two". Dualities within rear their heads in times of conflict particularly dramatic conflict... perhaps even catastrophic... the split in one's world can certainly create a chasm within as well as without. Which comes first, the chicken or the egg is yet another story. I just pray history isn't going to repeat itself too closely. I never ever thought I'd see in my own country the kind of madness that drove "my people" out of Europe...

I can't help it. I begin to wonder about the nature of Humanity itself, and once again remember how Anne Frank seemed to hold her romantic view of the world... through thick and thin. How did she do it?

I too am a Romantic, but I'm no longer certain, like Anne, that in spite of everything, people are truly good at heart.

What I do believe in is the highest potential within mankind. It's just that unfortunately I have seen in my long lifetime that the darkest abyss also, still exists. I can only pray, that those of us who are still capable of fierce dreaming are able to summon our better angels in such times of trouble... and make manifest that better world.

And this is why "The Fool" within who can and will continue the adventure of life itself must prevail. It's as simple as that!

Perhaps it's the perfect moment to return to my inner child, my Heavenly dreams, and my indomitable spirit in the face of these hard times...

Nov 13

Things come up at times like these. I can't help but think on them. And if things weren't so terribly dire, I might actually enjoy musing over the subject of such things as good and evil... something I've felt a horrible sense of anxiety over since childhood... and I suppose as a result, I never wanted to believe actual evil existed. I still don't. The concept just seems so far removed from my preferred philosophy, that the Sacred lies within all, as does Beauty. These days, however, I wonder... and I find myself coming full circle to a memory of long ago that may have pertinence... It has meaning for me at least.

I was... 6 or 7 at the time... and the experience remains a mystery lo these many years later, because honestly, I'm not certain if I'd had a waking dream or what... It was certainly a frighteningly mystical experience, however, and a darkly one. I recall being quite awake and alone one night while Tal and Mady were out. Of course, I have always had an active imagination, but I still believe we filter consciousness in our own unique way... there is information "out there" symbolically or otherwise... As Jean Houston would often say, we need to be careful to not pathologize too much... So here it is; on this particular evening when I was quite alone and quite awake, I caught something out of the corner of my eye by the living room window... And when I looked again, I saw the devil's face alongside Jesus Christ's floating by! Of course, it scared me so that I threw a blanket over my head and ran to my bed as fast as I could... And I had trouble walking past that living room window for some time to come, after that, and never spoke of it to anyone.

Of course, as an adult I am devoutly interested in things psychological and spiritual by nature, and so I have pondered this childhood experience over the years... but it really comes up now because despite my desire to push the notion away, we are living in the midst of much darkness, if not actual evil. I have absolutely no idea how I was privy to the images of the Devil or Christ at that tender age but I think for whatever reason, I was somehow open to a mystical symbol of the human dilemma that came to me in the light of day... not intellectually of course, but experientially and in my case, it might very well have been partly a psychic response to childhood crisis... However, what interests me is that the personal story is always a counterpart to the Universal...

And so, coming back to the times, I do think that if there is actual evil, it is born of the fusion of utter madness and the need for power... We've seen this in the world many times before... but what is the antidote? Is it love? And is understanding and forgiveness enough? I'm looking to heal this crazy world... and I'm just plain stymied.

Perhaps "the Goddess" will find the Sacred once more and with that, the mad "evil" of the times will be exorcised.

Nov. 16th

Could it be possible that things are getting worse?

Oh Goddess, Covid is completely out of hand.

Our hearts are breaking from the split in this World…

Divine One, we need you now…

Nov. 17th

I woke with an uncanny sense of hope… perhaps hope was delivered by the hand of the Goddess I prayed to yesterday. Isn't it funny how these things can work? Sometimes if we can ground a "higher" archetype, we can raise our frequency enough to see the light without losing ourselves. That grounding is key or spirituality itself becomes just one more escape mechanism. I may forever find myself chasing radiance, but only to embody it… or as Carl Jung put it, to make that which is unconscious conscious… Something each and every one of us might do well to attempt during these dark times! At least I can continue to work on that within myself. Perhaps therein lies the power of any agency I might have in the world at this time… I don't think it is magical thinking to remember the Gods and Goddesses or the Divine intelligence of the Universe itself…

Nov. 23rd

Today I am remembering President Kennedy… Lo these many years ago we lost him.

I was in 6th grade and remember it like it was yesterday. We were all so young but loved our beloved President of The United States of America… It was as if he fulfilled the ideal archetype of the Heroic leader. This was a time of American grace, hope and expansion. Whatever lay in the shadows, we were innocent to of course.

I remember the emotional chaos in the school hallway as if it was yesterday. I'll never forget… it was an American tragedy. Later that year, my mother died of a brain tumor at the age of 39.

In any event, I pray these days for a new and brighter paradigm… but as well, I pray for the kind of collective love, grace, and hope of the JFK Spirit we all once knew!

Nov. 24th

I'm not feeling well today but don't think too much about my personal health issues amidst the Universal health story. Now and then I do check in because despite it all, I hope to live to see a safer, more graceful time… I come to understand that we've seen violent energies of all sorts before and though it's quite the drama on so very many levels, the pendulum continues to swing… And Humanity keeps trying to get it right…

Carl Jung spoke of peoples… yes, masses of peoples gone mad as if possessed… as if caught by a Collective infection…

And Rollo May alluded to the idea that mass madness, unholy as it may be, can almost feel like the liberation of years of repression… This idea makes me think of what can happen and probably does, when one's inner Daimon lays dormant and unrealized… Inevitably it causes trouble or may even turn in on itself… The Daimon becomes the Demon… En mass it can feel almost apocalyptic in nature. The truth is, these days do feel dire… and I find myself relating more and more to the plight of my ancestors, only this time, there is no welcome mat on American soil that offers much grace even to those of us who live here!… It's really up to us to find it within…

I will say this however… in this dance of shadow and light, some hope has arrived and at least half of these United States are very relieved to know that the voting has been finalized, the states have certified Joe Biden as the President elect… And the GSA has finally opened their doors for the sake of a transition despite wild allegations of voter fraud…

There are, against many odds certain things the rest of us hold near and dear to our hearts however… and as dire as things are, I have to believe that we will see that new dawn… I still believe in good will for all and I mean *all* in the midst of mass bafflement!

Nov.26th. Thanksgiving morning

The Actor's nightmare: (I don't remember most of my dreams since I contracted Lyme disease so this was evidently an important one).

I should begin with this: Happy Thanksgiving 2020…

LIFE IS STILL BEAUTIFUL!

I *saw all the faces of family and friends come to see a great play in a majestic theatre. I didn't even know I was supposed to be opening a play, let alone having lines memorized... I didn't know I was in the play, let alone the star!*

It was taking place elsewhere as most openings are out of town and we were staying in a large Hotel. I went down the hallway once I received word of my strange circumstances... I was looking for help. I was looking for a fellow Actor, or stage hand, director... anyone affiliated with this... play. Finally, someone appeared and spoke with me. He told me I had little time to get ready and that he didn't understand why I wasn't even in costume. I proceeded to tell him I didn't have the script... Was never given the script and didn't know what on earth was going on... and that I'd need help somehow if at the last minute I was to possibly get the lines down. He rushed me to a rehearsal studio space on the floor above where many stage hands and techies were hanging out... and so we got started rehearsing act one. I realized he must have been an assistant director but he was perfectly helpful in any event.

My opening lines were single words of exclamations with pauses between each but still they had to feed me the words. After a few tries, not only was I able to recite them, but was able to feel them passionately... and that was obviously why I'd gotten that role in the first place... because my passion was a rare gift that moved people. It felt so good to exclaim the words, because for those moments in that rehearsal studio I spoke of the exquisite nature of the world... And the "rehearsal studio" went away while fireworks went off before the cosmos... Everyone applauded, but now I only had 5 minutes till show-time...

Of course, I'd only learned the opening passage and even that was already fading again. The assistant and I spoke of possible creative solutions but I was quite worried... I said," I'm in trouble. In terrible trouble... If I'm to go on, I will need the script..." And he repeated, "Yes, you will need the script... it's just that simple..."

And the craziest thing about this new play that I'd not even known I was supposed to have been rehearsed in, was that it was about exclaiming the beauty of all things to the Universe above... despite the terrible times we're living in.

As I'm writing this, tears are streaming. On one hand I'm saddened to say I've been grappling with fear of this plague and all who've suffered or died... and I feel worn out by this morality tale being played out in such an epic way these days. It is devastatingly depressing and I'm not one to avoid. Yes, I thank God I'm a creative... it's healing to be so of course... but I'm missing the rest of the players in the play... so very much.

I'd like to know a little more of the ecstasy of being alive again and let my exclamations be heard. I'd like that for all of us.

I am grateful for this dream, however, because it offered me a reminder of what's been forgotten... that life is still beautiful.

LIFE IS STILL BEAUTIFUL!

Happy Thanksgiving

Dec. 21

Dec. 21st brings the same ole' same ole' world chaos that's becoming the norm.

The collective Descent continues...

Jan. 5th

It's 5:00 am and I feel the need to jot down my dream before I lose it. There's a statement here for sure. I'd come "Home" after a time away on the road. But "Home" was hardly recognizable, as it had been ransacked and taken over. They, whoever they were put up garish wallpaper every-where and moved my furniture out of the house. One of the rooms appeared to be an office with overturned computers and such, and papers were strewn all over. My upset was at a fever pitch while I desperately tried as best I could to communicate that they had no right! No right to destroy my Home! They trashed my precious home that I'd created into a thing of beauty... a home that reflected nature, and was Sacred, but now had been completely ravaged and destroyed by them. When I woke, I felt trauma through to my core. And I thought of Donald Trump!

I don't think it's a far stretch to gather that the "Home" of my dream happens to be America... A Home that belongs to "We the People". No one has the right to think they can burn the house down... America, the land of the free is Sacred land built and nurtured with utmost care and we cannot allow anyone to destroy it!

Jan. 6th

OMG! Our Capitol! Our Democracy! Our Country! Our Home!

Little did I know how psychically in sync yesterday's dream would prove to be.

January 14th

I've not written in some time, I suppose, because things have become so terribly intense on all levels. I hardly know how to speak of it. It takes courage to decipher the world at large when your aim is to inspire rather than reflect for all to see, your feelings of fear and helplessness.

For anyone aware of the timeline you will know what occurred at the Capitol the day of the electoral count... and final certification of Joe Biden's win. It has been a devastating turn of events; as if life in America could get wilder. Pandora's box has been opened... and it has become exceedingly clear that extremists of all sorts, including white supremacists, were given oxygen these past 4 years. The result is beyond the imaginable. There are many stories about the agenda of those involved, but nonetheless the Capitol was stormed and it's lucky more people weren't killed... But I come full circle to the fascism my family had to bear. We really don't know what's to come. Now our Capitols across America will have to fend off National terrorism worse that any foreign attack on our soil... and it saddens me to no end that during this uncontrollable Pandemic, there is little coming together in grace, unity, and love, but rather in perhaps what history books will define as a Civil war if this hatred continues. Things have sped up since Trump was impeached for the second time, and the threats are simply outrageous. They say there are now more National Guardsmen protecting our Capitols than Afghanistan, Turkey, and Iraq combined.

Its hard to imagine, isn't it? I mean, how can we Americans accept our circumstances when we were the Heroes once upon a time and not so long ago? It seems we've landed in a new and troubling era and our role is certainly changing... And it all just feels so dark... but then I return to other more inherent truths that keep me going... and the mythic perspective of poets like Christopher Fry, who wrote, "A Sleep of Prisoners". May I remind you now of his magnificent notion that in the most horrific times, for all we know, we may just be entering the upstart Spring!

Jan. 20th

Inauguration Day. Oh yes, the dawn breaks and once again Radiance shines through. Things change. This is the nature of the Tao. This is the nature of life. Today was a day of rejoice and grace. The inauguration of our new President was the perfect medicine for those of us who were starting to lose faith... but you know what they say; as long as there is life there is hope.

May 10th

It's been 4 months since my last entry and naturally much has happened in the world, in my life, and I'm sure yours. I'll not be waiting another 11 years to pick up where I've left off however, because it's just about time to say goodbye, dear reader. I smile as I say this, but these memoirs and present-day journals have indeed felt like a conversation. And I can only hope that you, who have shown interest in my humble words have been moved or have at least learned a thing or two.

I've grappled with how to end my little book however, not because my story is incomplete... but because the times are so dramatic that I'd like to leave some final thoughts that might be helpful.

May we all be wholly human to our depths of our Souls.

May we remember the way of the inner child who lives in the realm of creativity and imagination.

We can do this... for it is surely not the time to give up on each other. Quite the contrary. It may very well be the time to believe once again in the power of the Human Heart.

PHOTO GALLERY
FAMILY, THEATRE & ART

GREAT-GRANDPARENTS
LEON & ANNA

MY GRANDPARENTS

HILDA

EDITH & BERNARD

MADO & PAPA SAM

MY PARENTS

WEDDING DAY
AUG.9 1987

SHANE & CHRISTINE
6/21/2018

ELEEMOSYNARY

LONG DAYS JOURNEY INTO NIGHT

JACQUES BREL IS ALIVE & WELL
& LIVING IN PARIS

THE UNITAUR

SQUARE ONE

SUDDENLY
LAST SUMMER

LA BELLA LUNA CIRQUE

205

CIRCLE MIRROR TRANSFORMATION

THE TWO
CHARACTER PLAY

NIGHT OUT

SISTERS ROSENZWEIG

THE JEWISH WIFE

POIGNANT IRRITATIONS

PAUL J CURTIS &
THE AMERICAN MIME THEATRE

WAYNE

ANNA

JANE

KAREN

EVAN

MY ART

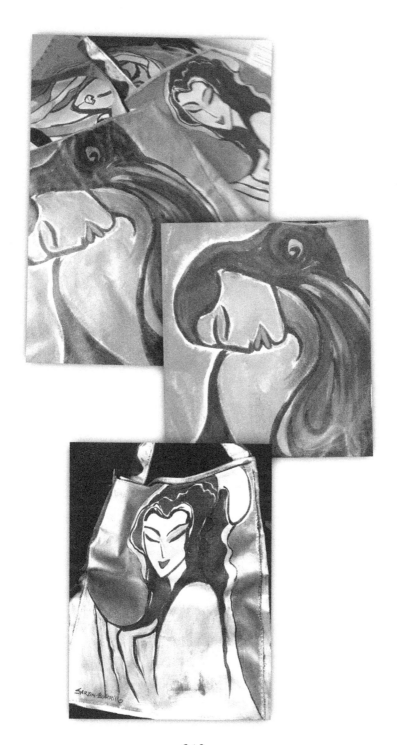

214

IN LOVING MEMORY

THE BLUE LADY
BY MADELINE SARZIN

"Dream on", said the Goddess to the Traveling Fool
"Dream on and envision the world anew
once more & once more & once more!"

ACKNOWLEDGMENTS

The recording of my story was a process that unfolded stage by stage… But while my original memoirs were written in journal form some time ago, this past year was dedicated to expanding and deepening it into a viable book. What came after a full year of literary solitude, was almost tantamount to working quite intimately with midwives and a most gracious support team. It was no longer a solo affair but rather a community effort and I would like to express my profound gratitude to everyone who helped along the way.

Those who read and endorse an author's pages are more appreciated than one might imagine. They are the first to respond to the hard work put in and if they indicate they are truly moved, the rest of the process becomes ever so much easier on the soul. I thank them all for their kind words.

I would also like to acknowledge Lori Hansen who transcribed the original pages 11 years ago and Paul Page who proof read my manuscript (I thank God he did).

And, thank you, Denny Bitte for allowing the use of your exquisite photo for the cover of "Chasing Radiance". I think it perfectly captures the mystical essence of memories and reflections returning to the light of day.

Finally, I wish to thank one of my oldest dearest friends, Karen Neville, who worked closely with me on the design of the interior of the book as well as the cover. I would never have been able to do it without her. This is the third project we've worked on together. And not only have I turned to her because she is a graphic designer by profession, but because time and again our creative ventures have rekindled our very precious bond that began long ago. Thank you, dear Karen. You are a true friend of my Soul. And working with you on "Chasing Radiance" has been a pure joy!

ABOUT THE AUTHOR

Erica Sarzin-Borrillo has spent her life in the integrative arts as a painter, healer, and performing artist. She began a form of Soul writing some years ago as a ritual that led to poetry, philosophical essays and conversations with the Beloved.
Ms. Sarzin-Borrillo is a Visionary writer and author of "The House of Gathering", and "Oracle of the Divine Feminine."

For more information about

Erica Sarzin-Borrillo
Go to www.ericasarzinborrillo.com
Or www.mythichealingarts.com

Email: ericact@msn.com

Made in the USA
Las Vegas, NV
20 July 2021